THE BARBECUE BOOK

THE BARBECUE BOOK

AWESOME RECIPES TO FIRE UP YOUR BARBECUE

This edition published by Parragon Books Ltd in 2015
LOVE FOOD is an imprint of Parragon Books Ltd

Parragon Books Ltd
Chartist House
15—17 Trim Street
Bath BA1 1HA, UK
www.parragon.com/lovefood

ISBN 978-1-4723-7839-2

Printed in China

New recipes and home economy by Lincoln Jefferson
New photography by Mike Cooper
New text by Robin Donovan
Edited and project managed by Cheryl Warner
Designed by Lexi L'Esteve
Illustrations by Scott Rhodes, courtesy of The Bright Agency

Notes for the Reader
This book uses both metric and imperial measurements. Follow the same units of
measurement throughout; do not mix metric and imperial. All spoon measurements
are level: teaspoons are assumed to be 5 ml, and tablespoons are assumed to be
15 ml. Unless otherwise stated, milk is assumed to be full fat, eggs and individual
vegetables are medium, and pepper is freshly ground black pepper. Unless otherwise
stated, all root vegetables should be peeled prior to using.

Garnishes, decorations and serving suggestions are all optional and not necessarily
included in the recipe ingredients or method. The times given are an approximate
guide only. Preparation times differ according to the techniques used by different
people and the cooking times may also vary from those given. Optional ingredients,
variations or serving suggestions have not been included in the time calculations.

Contents

INTRODUCTION   6

Vegetables   18
Beef   38
Pork & Lamb   58
Chicken & Turkey   78
Fish & Seafood   96
Sides, Drinks & Desserts   110

Index   128

Bring On The Barbecue!

Food and fire combine to create one of the best things in life —
barbecue. Add a patio full of friends, a pair of barbecue tongs
in one hand and a cold beer in the other, and it doesn't get much
better. Grilling food — meat, veggies, even seafood or fruit — over
hot coals brings a deep, primal sense of satisfaction and pleasure.
And nothing brings out the natural flavours of meat and vegetables
quite the way cooking them on the grill does — whether using a high-
heat, fast-grilling method, low-and-slow cooking or smoking. Not to
mention, barbecuing is fast, delicious and easy to clean up.

A GRILL FOR EVERY PERSON, PLACE AND OCCASION

The array of grills on the market these days is mind-boggling — gas,
charcoal, electric, gigantic or small enough to carry to the beach. Whether
you opt for a full-sized charcoal grill, a balcony-sized electric grill or a
quick-cleaning gas grill is a personal choice and depends on your barbecuing
priorities. Whether you want intense smoky flavour or a system that will
allow you to cook up a delicious and healthy meal any place, any time, there
is a grill that is just right.

CHARCOAL, WOOD OR GAS?

If it's smoky, chargrilled flavour that draws you to barbecuing, a charcoal
or wood grill is your best bet. If, however, convenience, speed and easy
clean-up are most important to you, a gas grill cannot be beaten. The
recipes in this book are designed to be cooked on any of these types of
grills so whichever you decide, you can't go wrong.

CHARCOAL GRILLS AND KETTLES

Charcoal grills come in many shapes and sizes. The kettle grill is the
standard-style grill. Round with a deep bowl, a kettle grill has a grate
in the bottom that the charcoal sits on and, above that, a grill where the
food is cooked. Simple and functional, this type of grill is the perfect
solution for the frequent or occasional barbecue cook because it is sturdy,
inexpensive and versatile. You can use a kettle grill for high-heat
grilling, slower indirect cooking (what's known in grilling circles as true
barbecuing), and even as a smoker.

Charcoal grills also come in small, portable tabletop versions, as well as
large rectangular versions. Whichever you choose, look for one with sturdy
legs and adjustable vents that give you the ability to control the heat of
your fire.

Charcoal briquettes, which are manufactured from wood by-products, are easy to find (they're available in pretty much any supermarket), inexpensive and easy to transport, making them perhaps more convenient than wood. Easy-light varieties make using charcoal more convenient than ever — with these, you won't even need lighter fluid.

Lump charcoal, on the other hand, is a more natural form of charcoal. To make it, logs are burned in an oxygen-free environment and they are generally made without a lot of additives (meaning you won't get even a hint of lighter fluid's flavour in your food), leading purists to choose them over briquettes.

WOOD-FIRED GRILLS

Charcoal grills can also be used as wood-fired barbecues. The appeal of grilling over wood is that it adds flavour and, many think, is less polluting than charcoal. You can buy bags of wood chips and/or large hunks of various types of wood. Wood can be a lot more finicky than charcoal to cook with as you have to contend with many different factors — such as how dry the wood is or how big the pieces are, both of which affect how hot or fast they burn, how much smoke they put out, and what flavour they impart.

Pellet grills use small pellets made by compressing sawdust, rather than whole pieces of wood. These pellets come in a variety of 'flavours' and burn cleanly and quickly to a fine ash. The small size and easy-to-control burn of the pellets means that these types of grills offer the best of both worlds. You get ease of use and convenience similar to a gas grill with the added smoky flavour of a hardwood grilling.

GAS GRILLS

Gas grills are ideal for people who want to be able to cook up a meal quickly and enjoy minimal clean-up. The biggest benefits of gas grills are that they heat up in minutes with the turn of a dial, have easily controlled heat, clean up easily, and are less polluting than charcoal. The downside of gas grills is that they don't work well for smoking and don't impart that delectable smoky, chargrilled flavour. Some barbecue purists turn their noses up at gas grills, but they are practical.

Like charcoal grills, gas grills come in a wide range of styles from small portable models to gigantic garden behemoths capable of grilling up meals for a crowd. Whichever size of gas grill you choose, go for the best quality you can afford.

Having multiple burners, too, is key to being able to control your heat and have versatility in your cooking abilities. Having two burners allows you to use both direct and indirect heat. Having three or more burners gives you even more heat control. Angled metal plates over the burners keep the heat evenly dispersed and prevent flare-ups. If you want to combine both the convenience of a gas grill with the smoky flavour-imparting abilities of a charcoal one, look for a gas grill with lava rocks. These are hard to find and more expensive, but if you're handy, you might be able to rig a standard gas grill to get the same effect.

ELECTRIC GRILLS

A new breed of outdoor electric grills has hit the market in recent years, opening up barbecuing possibilities for even those with no outdoor space save a small balcony or patio. While they don't have the power of either charcoal or gas, if it's your only choice, it will certainly do.

SMOKERS

To make delicious smoked meats, really all you need is a basic charcoal grill, but if you want to really impress your friends, some additional equipment is needed. Fortunately, there are plenty of stand-alone smokers and smoker attachments to choose from. With these, you can produce fantastic smoked foods without having to hover over the machine all day checking and adjusting the temperature, adding wood chips, or basting the meat. A good smoker or smoker attachment lets you set it and forget it and still put a great tasting meal on the table at the end of the day. You can also adapt charcoal, gas and electric grills for smoking (see right).

SMOKER ATTACHMENTS

The simplest way to equip yourself for barbecue smoking is a smoker attachment that extends the abilities of the grill you already have. If you've got a kettle grill, for instance, you can probably buy an inexpensive attachment that will virtually turn it into a stand-alone smoker.

Many gas grills can be upgraded with a smoker box attachment, a heavy, vented metal container that holds wood chips and enables you to smoke foods on the gas grill you already have.

VERTICAL GAS SMOKERS

Vertical gas smokers are less versatile, since they only do one thing, but they do a great job of smoking meats and are easy to use.

DRUM-, BULLET-, OR CONE-SHAPED SMOKERS

Charcoal-fired drum, bullet, and cone- or egg-shaped smokers are more expensive, but they create great smoky flavour and are easy to keep at a low temperature, which is essential if you want smoky flavour without drying out your food.

If you're serious about smoking, pellet smokers — grills fuelled by burning small pellets of compressed hardwood sawdust — are the way to go. They are easy to use, hold a temperature well and create a distinctive, yet still delicate, smoky flavour.

Get Things Cookin'

No matter what type of grill you choose and whether you're using gas, wood or charcoal, barbecuing is a fun and easy way to make tasty meals. Using three main methods — direct-heat cooking, indirect-heat cooking and smoking — you can use your barbecue or grill to make a head-spinning, mouth-watering array of foods.

DIRECT-HEAT COOKING

Direct-heat grilling refers to the intense, high-heat grilling most people use to sear a steak, quick-cook burgers to a beautiful medium-rare, or grill salmon just until it has those nice black grill marks and is cooked through but still moist and tender in the middle. Use direct-heat cooking when you want to sear the food quickly, give it a nice charred flavour and caramelize the outside without drying out the centre. Ideally, foods that you intend to cook over direct heat should be seasoned with dry spices or spice rubs. They can also be marinated, but if you use a glaze that contains sugar, wait until the end of the cooking time to brush it on to prevent the sugar from burning.

The direct-heat grilling method is ideal for steaks, chops, burgers, fish, shellfish, chicken, sausages and vegetables.

In direct cooking, the food is cooked directly above the heat source. With charcoal, this means simply placing the pile of hot coals under the area where you plan to cook. You can even use one side of the grill for direct-heat cooking by pushing all of the coals to that side, but leaving the other side of the grill open for indirect cooking. To use direct-heat cooking on a gas, wood-fired or electric grill, simply place the food directly over the burners or heat source.

No matter how much of the grill you intend to use for direct-heat cooking, it's a good idea to oil the grate to keep your food from sticking. To oil the grate, soak a folded paper towel with oil and then use a grill-cleaning brush or long-handled barbecue tongs to rub the oil-soaked towel over the grate until it is nicely coated with oil. Note that the oil will smoke a bit as you do this, but this is perfectly fine.

Direct-heat cooking, then, is accomplished by placing the food onto the oiled grate directly over very hot coals or hot burners, cooking for a few minutes on one side, then turning and cooking for a few minutes on the other.

INDIRECT-HEAT COOKING

Indirect-heat cooking is a 'low-and-slow' method of barbecuing where you place the food on a hot grill, but not directly on top of the heat source. Additionally, the grill's cover is kept closed during cooking to keep the heat in. When using charcoal or wood, you simply push the hot coals or wood to the side to make a space on the grill that does not have the heat directly under it. On a gas grill, you can accomplish the same thing by heating up the grill with all of the burners on and then turning off one or two of them to make a space where you can cook the food without it being directly over the heat source.

This method is best for longer-cooking cuts of meat, such as roasts, whole chickens or turkeys, and other slow-cooking foods.

As in direct-heat cooking, it's a good idea to oil the grate to keep your food from sticking. Heat the grill first, then move the coals away from your cooking area or cut off the burners in that area, soak a folded paper towel with oil and then use a grill-cleaning brush or long-handled barbecue tongs to rub the oil-soaked towel over the grate until it is nicely coated with oil.

SMOKING

Smoking is a general term for using heat and smoke (from wood and/or charcoal) to cook food. Food is placed onto the grill, which is then closed and filled with heat and smoke (see pages 8 and 9 for smokers and smoker attachments). This process cooks and flavours the meat simultaneously. Smoking is generally done at lower temperatures, which allows the foods time to absorb the smoky flavour while still cooking at a steady enough temperature to safely keep bacteria at bay.

Turn Up the Heat

Here is how to start and heat up various types of barbecue.

COOKING WITH WOOD

To build a wood fire, follow these simple steps.

1. Make a small pile of twigs and paper scraps on the charcoal grate of your barbecue.

2. Over the twig pile, construct a 'teepee' of small sticks, balancing the sticks against each other so that they stand up with room for air to circulate underneath.

3. Light a match and hold it to the twigs and paper scraps until they ignite. Light the sticks in several places.

4. When the sticks catch fire, begin adding increasingly larger pieces, waiting for them to catch fire before adding more.

5. Once you've got a good strong fire, begin adding the larger logs, being sure to lean them against each other, always leaving room for air to circulate underneath.

6. Once the fire is blazing, let it go for about 40 minutes for a really hot heat source. Once the logs are glowing and hot, use a poker, barbecue tongs or a long stick to distribute them as you wish under the grill.

CHARCOAL BRIQUETTES IN A CHIMNEY STARTER

To light charcoal briquettes, a chimney starter — a cylindrical device that allows you to light your briquettes quickly and without lighter fluid — is highly recommended. If you've got one, put it on the charcoal grate of your barbecue, fill the bottom section with wadded-up newspaper and fill the top section with charcoal briquettes. Using a match or lighter, ignite the newspaper. Once the coals catch fire, give them about 20 minutes to get hot. Once all of the briquettes are coated with white ash they are ready to spread out. Carefully tip them out of the chimney onto the charcoal grate and spread the coals out using a long stick or barbecue tongs.

CHARCOAL BRIQUETTES WITH LIGHTER FLUID

If using regular, untreated charcoal briquettes without a chimney starter, make a pile of the briquettes on the charcoal grate of your barbecue. Douse the pile with lighter fluid and give it a few minutes to soak in (while you wait, place the cap securely on the lighter fluid container and place it at a safe distance from the barbecue). Using a match or lighter, light the briquettes in several places and let them burn for 30–40 minutes, until they are all glowing red and covered with white ash. Once they're hot enough, spread them out for an even cooking area using barbecue tongs or a long stick.

EASY-LIGHT BRIQUETTES

Easy-light briquettes are pretreated with lighter fluid, making them convenient and easy to use. Simply pile pretreated briquettes on the charcoal grate of your barbecue and light with a match. The briquettes will be ready for grilling when they are glowing and mostly covered with white ash, which will take about 30–40 minutes. Once they're hot enough, spread them out for an even cooking area using barbecue tongs or a long stick.

LIGHTING A GAS GRILL

The most important thing to remember when lighting a gas grill is to do so with the lid open. Otherwise there is the potential for gas to build up inside. In this case, sudden ignition could lead to a dangerous explosion. Beyond that, every gas grill is a bit different so simply follow the manufacturers' instructions for lighting and preheating.

LOW, MEDIUM AND HOT HEAT

Surely one of the most important elements of a good barbecue is getting the heat just right. If you don't, then no matter how good your recipe or ingredients are, your results could be disastrous. But this simple technique will prevent culinary mishaps caused by a too hot or too cool fire.

To roughly determine how hot a fire is, place your hand just above the grill and count seconds (for example 'one Mississippi, two Mississippi...'). When a fire is hot (hot heat or 230°C–290°C/450°F–550°F), you'll need to pull your hand away in 1–2 seconds. With a medium fire (medium heat or 160°C–180°C /325°F–350°F), you'll be able to keep your hand there for about 3 seconds. With a low fire (low heat or 110°C–120°C/225°F–250°F), you can keep your hand there for 4–5 seconds.

In this book, the recipes state to preheat to certain temperatures. These
temperatures are:

Low: 110°C—120°C/225°F—250°F
Medium-low: 130°C—150°C/260°F—300°F
Medium: 160°C—180°C/325°F—350°F
Medium-hot: 190°C—220°C/375°F—425°F
Hot: 230°C—290°C/450°F—550°F

Please check the barbecue temperature is correct using a thermometer before
starting to cook for absolute accuracy.

BASIC GEAR YOU NEED

Once you've got your grill and fuel sorted, there are just a few more tools
you'll need to invest in. You can find any number of fun barbecue tools
that may enhance your barbecue, but here is a list of absolutely essential
barbecue tools:

TONGS

A nice sturdy pair of long-handled tongs is essential for manoeuvering hot
food around the grill. Stainless steel, spring-loaded tongs are good for
durability and ease of use. A second pair of tongs reserved for moving
around hot coals and other non-food items is also extremely handy.

SKEWERS

There are really two choices to consider when choosing skewers. The first
is disposable bamboo skewers. The benefits of these are that they are
inexpensive and don't need to be cleaned. Of course, their disposability can
also be seen as a negative. Another downside is that they need to be pre-
soaked in water for 30 minutes before placing on a hot grill to prevent them
from burning.

The second choice is long metal skewers with a flat-blade design (as opposed
to cylindrical metal sticks). The blade design prevents food from turning on
the skewer when you attempt to turn the skewers over on the grill. The fact
that these are reusable is a benefit, but of course, that means they must be
cleaned after each use. Look for metal skewers with heat-resistant handles,
otherwise prepare to use oven mitts to avoid burning yourself on the hot
metal when you turn the skewers over on the grill.

BASTER
A long-handled, natural fibre brush (stay away from anything that might melt at high heat!) or a mop-style baster is useful for basting meats with marinade as they cook.

WIRE BRUSH
A long-handled wire brush is essential for cleaning the grill.

THERMOMETER
This is very helpful for checking that the barbecue has reached the desired temperature before cooking.

MEAT THERMOMETER
An instant-read meat thermometer is extremely useful for checking the temperature of meat to make sure it is done. This is especially important with large cuts of meat, such as roasts or whole chickens or turkeys.

Is It Done Yet?

Now that you've invested in a handsome grill, outfitted yourself with essential barbecue gear and are ready to get cooking, let's just take a minute to talk about safety. Cooking food until it is properly done is crucial for avoiding food poisoning, but knowing when food reaches this point can be a tricky business. There are a couple of different ways to test meat for doneness.

WHOLE OR JOINTS OF CHICKEN OR TURKEY

To check a whole chicken for doneness, you can insert a skewer into the thickest part of one of the thighs. If it's done, the juices should run clear. Wiggling a drumstick is another method. If the chicken is done, the drumstick will turn easily and feel very loose.

BURGERS, SAUSAGES AND PORK

These should be cooked until the centre is no longer pink and the juices run clear.

FISH

It's relatively easy to tell when fish is cooked through. Simply press on the fish at its thickest point. If it is done, the flesh will flake easily.

PRAWNS

Cook until they are fully opaque and turn pink.

OYSTERS, MUSSELS AND CLAMS

Discard any whose shells are open before cooking. Cook until the shells open fully and discard any whose shells do not open after sufficient cooking.

THERMOMETER METHOD

If you want to be really safe, opt for the more scientific thermometer method. This method is more or less essential when you are cooking large cuts of meat such as roasts, legs of lamb or whole turkeys. Use a digital, instant-read thermometer inserted at the thickest part of the meat (be sure it is not touching bone) and refer to the chart below.

TYPE OF MEAT	RARE	MEDIUM-RARE	MEDIUM	WELL-DONE
BEEF	51°C/125°F	65°C/145°F	70°C/160°F	77°C/170°F (OR HIGHER)
LAMB	51°C/125°F	65°C/145°F	70°C/160°F	77°C/170°F (OR HIGHER)
PORK	N/A	N/A	70°C/160°F	77°C/170°F (OR HIGHER)
CHICKEN AND TURKEY	N/A	N/A	70°C/160°F	77°C/170°F (OR HIGHER)
DUCK	51°C/125°F	65°C/145°F	70°C/160°F	77°C/170°F (OR HIGHER)

Please also check current government guidelines for the latest information on cooking temperatures.

GENERAL FOOD SAFETY

Use common sense and basic food safety rules when it comes to preparing and storing food outside. For instance, you should always wash your hands before handling food, whether you are barbecuing in your garden or cooking in the kitchen.

Bacteria can grow and multiply in any type of food and they thrive at temperatures between 5°C/40°F and 60°C/140°F. Keep food — especially meat, poultry and seafood — in the refrigerator or a cooler (below 5°C/40°F) until ready to prepare for cooking.

Thoroughly thaw frozen meat, poultry, or fish before grilling to ensure even cooking.

Always keep raw meat, fish or poultry apart from cooked foods. If you use utensils or dishes to handle raw meat, wash them thoroughly before using them for cooked food.

SAFE GRILLING

Fire is a dangerous beast and every time you light up your grill, you are welcoming it into your garden. There's no reason your family can't live peacefully with it, but a few precautions are in order.

1.   Have a fire extinguisher nearby and know how to use it.
2.   Don't put your grill or smoker too close to buildings, trees, foliage or other flammable materials. Check the instructions for minimum distances.
3.   Make sure that one person is in charge of watching the grill at all times.
4.   Minimize flare-ups by keeping your grill or smoker clean. Clean grates completely with a wire brush, empty ashes and brush all surfaces clean after every use.
5.   Inspect any grill, especially a gas grill, regularly to make sure there are no blockages or other problems that could cause a dangerous situation.
6.   If using charcoal with lighter fluid, be extremely careful. Never add lighter fluid to burning coals and, of course, keep the container of lighter fluid tightly sealed and far away from the fire.
7.   Keep children a good distance from hot surfaces and any equipment or fuel.

GET GRILLIN'

Once you've got your grill, your tools and your methods sorted, it's time to fire up that bad boy and start cooking. The recipes here are designed to be easy to use, but they never skimp on flavour. So what are you waiting for? Fire up that 'cue, crack a cold one and get cooking!

Chapter 1
VEGETABLES

Cheddar & Dill Pickle
Stuffed Jackets

 SERVES 4

 PREP: 20 MINS

 COOK: 1 HOUR 10 MINS

INGREDIENTS

4 jacket potatoes

4 tbsp olive oil

1 tsp salt

CHEDDAR & PICKLE FILLING

2 tbsp soured cream

1 small red onion, chopped

100 g/3½ oz strong Cheddar cheese, grated

55 g/2 oz dill pickles, or gherkins, chopped

½ tsp salt

1 tsp pepper

1. Prepare the barbecue for indirect cooking and preheat to medium.

2. Place the jacket potatoes on a baking tray. Drizzle with the oil and sprinkle over the salt.

3. Place on the barbecue grill with the lid on for an hour, or until the jacket is soft to the touch. Remove from the barbecue and leave to cool slightly.

4. Cut the jackets into halves and scoop out the flesh. Place the flesh in a bowl and mash lightly. Now add the filling ingredients and mix well with a wooden spoon.

5. Divide the mixture between the jacket skins and then put back in the baking tray. Place on the barbecue grill and cook with the lid on for 10 minutes, or until lightly golden and bubbling. Serve immediately.

TRY EXPERIMENTING WITH
DIFFERENT CHEESES, SUCH
AS GORGONZOLA.

Portobello Mushrooms

★ SERVES 4 ★

PREP: 15 MINS

COOK: 5 MINS

INGREDIENTS

1 kg/2 lb 4 oz
Portobello mushrooms

5 tbsp olive oil

1 tsp salt

1 tsp pepper

4 garlic cloves, chopped

small bunch of fresh
parsley, chopped

500 g/1 lb 2 oz
Gorgonzola, sliced

1. Prepare the barbecue for direct cooking and preheat to hot.

2. Remove and discard the stems from the mushrooms. Drizzle the mushrooms with the olive oil, then sprinkle with the salt and pepper.

3. Add the garlic and parsley, and top the mushrooms with the Gorgonzola slices.

4. Place on the barbecue grill and cook, cheese-side up, with the lid on for 5 minutes, or until the mushrooms are cooked and the cheese has melted.

THESE CAN BE MADE IN
ADVANCE AND KEPT IN THE
FRIDGE FOR UP TO A DAY.

Grilled Cajun Vegetables
with Parmesan Grits

★ SERVES 4 ★

PREP: 20 MINS

COOK: 30 MINS

INGREDIENTS

4 tbsp olive oil

1 tsp salt

1 tbsp Cajun spice

2 courgettes, halved lengthways

1 aubergine, quartered lengthways

100 g/3½ oz baby corn

1 red pepper, sliced

1 yellow pepper, sliced

20 g/¾ oz Parmesan cheese, grated

GRITS

1 litre/1¾ pints whole milk

55 g/2 oz butter

350 g/12 oz coarse cornmeal

100 g/3½ oz Parmesan cheese, grated

1 tsp salt

1 tsp pepper

1. To make the grits, place the milk and butter in a medium, heavy-based stainless steel saucepan and warm over a medium heat. When the milk and butter have started to boil, whisk in all the cornmeal. Turn down the heat and stir with a wooden spoon for 10 minutes, or until the cornmeal resembles a light mash consistency. Remove from the heat, beat in the Parmesan and sprinkle with the salt and pepper. Cover and leave in a warm place.

2. Prepare the barbecue for direct cooking and preheat to medium-hot.

3. In a large bowl, mix together the oil, salt and Cajun spice. Add the courgettes, aubergine, baby corn and peppers and mix well to coat thoroughly.

4. Cook the vegetables on the barbecue grill for 4 minutes on each side, or until they are slightly charred but soft to the touch. Serve the vegetables over the grits. Sprinkle with the Parmesan and serve immediately.

TRY USING GRITS AS AN
ALTERATIVE TO MASH — IT'S
GREAT WITH BUTTER, CREAM,
CHEESE AND HERBS.

Mediterranean
Grilled Aubergines

 SERVES 4

 PREP: 15 MINS

 COOK: 15 MINS

INGREDIENTS

GRILLED AUBERGINES

2 large aubergines

4 tbsp olive oil

1 tsp salt

1 tsp pepper

TAHINI YOGURT

2 tbsp Greek yogurt

1 tbsp tahini

1 garlic clove, crushed

juice of 1 lemon

salt and pepper, to taste

30 g/1 oz butter

100 g/3½ oz pine nuts

handful of rocket

100 g/3½ oz raisins

2 tbsp extra virgin olive oil, for drizzling

1. Cut the aubergines in half lengthways, then score the flesh on a slight angle into diamond shapes.

2. Drizzle the aubergines with the olive oil and sprinkle with the salt and pepper.

3. Prepare the barbecue for direct cooking and preheat to medium-hot.

4. To make the yogurt, mix together the yogurt, tahini, garlic and lemon juice in a small bowl. Season with salt and pepper.

5. Lay the aubergines on the barbecue grill, skin-side down, and cook for 7 minutes, or until the flesh is golden and soft to the touch. Turn over and cook for another 7 minutes.

6. Meanwhile, heat the butter in a small frying pan over a medium heat. Add the pine nuts and toast until they are a light golden colour. When the aubergines are cooked, divide between four plates and serve with the tahini yogurt, rocket, pine nuts and raisins. Drizzle with extra virgin olive oil and serve.

WHEN USING SALAD LEAVES,
ALWAYS GIVE THEM A GOOD
SOAK IN WATER TO CLEAN AND
REVITALIZE THE LEAVES.

Squash & Polenta
Burgers

★ SERVES 4-6 ★

PREP: 25 MINS
+ CHILLING

COOK:
45-50 MINS

INGREDIENTS

450 g/1 lb butternut squash (225 g/8 oz after peeling and deseeding), cut into chunks

150 ml/5 fl oz water

85 g/3 oz instant polenta

115 g/4 oz celeriac, grated

6 spring onions, finely chopped

115 g/4 oz pecan nuts, chopped

55 g/2 oz freshly grated Parmesan cheese

2 tbsp chopped fresh mixed herbs

2 tbsp wholemeal flour

2 tbsp sunflower oil, plus extra for oiling

salt and pepper

TO SERVE

burger buns

salad leaves

tomato slices

tomato ketchup

1. Cook the butternut squash in a saucepan of boiling water for 15—20 minutes, or until tender. Drain and finely chop or mash. Set aside.

2. Place the water in a separate saucepan and bring to the boil. Slowly pour in the polenta in a steady stream and cook over a gentle heat, stirring, for 5 minutes, or until thick.

3. Remove the saucepan from the heat and stir in the butternut squash, celeriac, spring onions, pecan nuts, cheese, herbs and salt and pepper to taste. Mix well, then shape into four to six burger patties. Coat the burgers in the flour, cover and leave to chill for 1 hour.

4. Prepare the barbecue for direct cooking and preheat to medium-hot.

5. Grease the barbecue grill. Lightly brush the burgers with the oil and cook for 5—6 minutes on each side, or until cooked through. Transfer to serving plates and serve immediately in the burger buns with the salad leaves, tomato slices and tomato ketchup.

THESE DELICIOUS VEGGIE
BURGERS MAKE A GREAT
ALTERNATIVE TO THE STANDARD
BEAN BURGER.

Satay Tofu Salad

SERVES 4

PREP: 20 MINS + MARINATING

COOK: 20 MINS

INGREDIENTS

800 g/1 lb 12 oz extra-firm tofu

MARINADE

2 tbsp soy sauce

2 tbsp sesame oil

2 tbsp mirin (rice wine), sake, sherry or white wine

SATAY SAUCE

80 g/2¾ oz smooth peanut butter

125 ml/4 fl oz coconut milk

2 tbsp soy sauce

2 tbsp soft light brown sugar

2 tbsp hot water, plus extra if needed

juice of 1 lime

2 tsp chilli paste, plus extra to taste

1 garlic clove, finely ground

1 tbsp grated fresh ginger

TO SERVE

lettuce leaves

red and orange pepper strips

cucumber strips

whole basil leaves

1. Slice the tofu into 2.5-cm/1-inch thick slabs and pat very dry with kitchen paper, pressing to release the excess moisture.

2. To make the marinade, combine the soy sauce, oil and mirin in a large bowl. Add the tofu and turn to coat. Marinate for at least 30 minutes and up to 8 hours (refrigerate if marinating for longer than 30 minutes).

3. To make the satay sauce, combine the peanut butter, coconut milk, soy sauce, sugar, water, lime juice, chilli paste, garlic and ginger in a bowl and stir to mix well. Add more water, a teaspoon or two at a time, if needed to reach the desired consistency.

4. Prepare the barbecue for direct cooking and preheat to medium-hot. Baste the tofu with some satay sauce, place on the barbecue grill and cook for about 10 minutes on each side, or until golden brown. Cut into strips.

5. Serve the tofu on a bed of lettuce leaves, with the pepper and cucumber strips and basil leaves. Serve immediately with extra satay sauce for drizzling.

THIS TOFU SALAD IS A GREAT ADDITION TO THE BARBECUE FOR ANY VEGETARIAN GUESTS OR FOR ANYONE ON A DIET.

Grilled Stuffed Peppers

SERVES 4

PREP: 20 MINS

COOK: 35–40 MINS

INGREDIENTS

4 large red peppers

FILLING

2 tbsp olive oil

1 small onion, diced

2 courgettes, diced

1 tsp salt

1 tsp ground cumin

425 g/15 oz canned chickpeas, drained and rinsed

200 g/7 oz freshly cooked brown rice

zest and juice of 1 lemon

2 tbsp finely chopped fresh mint

115 g/4 oz feta cheese, crumbled

1. Prepare the barbecue for indirect cooking and preheat to medium.

2. To make the filling, heat the oil in a heavy-based frying pan over a medium-high heat. Add the onion, courgettes and salt and cook for about 5 minutes, stirring occasionally, until the onion is translucent and the courgettes are beginning to brown. Stir in the cumin and chickpeas and cook, stirring, for a further 1 minute. Remove from the heat and leave to cool for a few minutes.

3. Combine the courgette and chickpea mixture in a large bowl with the rice, lemon zest and juice, mint and cheese. Stir to mix well.

4. Carefully slice off the tops of the red peppers, then core and deseed them. Stuff them with the rice mixture, then replace the tops and secure them with cocktail sticks or skewers.

5. Place the peppers on the barbecue grill on their sides and cook, covered, for about 25–30 minutes, turning every 5 minutes, until soft and just beginning to char. Serve immediately.

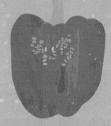

THIS TASTY DISH WILL DELIGHT
BOTH MEAT EATERS AND
VEGETARIANS ALIKE.

Baked Sweet Potatoes
with Salsa

 SERVES 4

 PREP: 20 MINS

 COOK: 1 HOUR

INGREDIENTS

4 sweet potatoes,
about 350 g/12 oz each

1 tbsp olive oil,
for rubbing

large knob of butter

2 tbsp chopped fresh
coriander

100 g/3½ oz grated feta
cheese or other salty
white cheese

salt and pepper

SALSA

3 tomatoes, deseeded and
finely diced

1 small red onion,
finely diced

½–1 small green chilli,
deseeded and finely diced

3 tbsp chopped fresh
coriander

juice of 1 lime

1. Prepare the barbecue for indirect cooking and preheat to medium. Use some kitchen paper to rub the potatoes with a little olive oil and sprinkle with salt to coat lightly.

2. Tightly wrap the potatoes in pieces of double-thickness aluminium foil and place on the barbecue grill for about 1 hour.

3. Meanwhile, combine the salsa ingredients in a bowl. Add a little salt to taste. Leave to stand at room temperature to let the flavours develop.

4. When the potatoes are cooked, cut them open, fork the flesh and mix in a little butter, salt and pepper, and most of the coriander. Sprinkle with the cheese and the remaining coriander. Serve immediately with the salsa spooned over the top.

SWEET POTATOES MAKE A TASTY ALTERNATIVE TO NORMAL JACKET POTATOES AND CONTAIN LESS CARBS.

Creamed Spinach

SERVES 4

PREP: 10 MINS

COOK: 15-20 MINS

INGREDIENTS

4 tbsp olive oil

1 large shallot, diced

2 garlic cloves, crushed

100 g/3½ oz smoked bacon lardons

1 large carrot, diced

150 g/5½ oz celeriac, diced

½ tsp salt

1 tsp pepper

200 ml/7 fl oz double cream

250 g/9 oz fresh spinach

1. Heat the oil in a large saucepan over a medium heat. Add the shallot, garlic, lardons, carrot and celeriac. Sweat the vegetables with a lid on for 10 minutes, or until softened, stirring every now and then.

2. Season with the salt and pepper. Add the double cream and simmer the mixture until it is reduced by half.

3. Meanwhile, bring a medium saucepan of water to the boil. Blanch the spinach for a few seconds, then drain and run under cold water until the spinach is cooled. Squeeze out the excess water from the spinach, then add to the creamed vegetables. Stir to combine and serve immediately.

FOR A HEALTHIER VERSION,
REPLACE THE DOUBLE CREAM
WITH LIGHT OR SOYA CREAM.

Chapter 2
BEEF

Beef Brisket
with Soy & Ginger Rub

 ☆ SERVES 6-8 ☆

PREP: 20 MINS
+ MARINATING
+ RESTING

COOK: 10 HOURS

INGREDIENTS

2 kg/4 lb 8 oz beef
brisket

SOY & GINGER RUB

100 g/3½ oz soft brown
sugar

150 ml/5 fl oz light soy
sauce

150 ml/5 fl oz mirin

2 tbsp Korean chilli
bean paste

4 garlic cloves, crushed

55 g/2 oz fresh ginger,
sliced

1 tsp pepper

1 tsp Sichuan
peppercorns

3 star anise

1 cinnamon stick

1. To make the rub, mix all the ingredients together in a large bowl. Add the brisket and stir until the beef is coated thoroughly.

2. Place the brisket in a tight-fitting non-metallic dish and pour over any remaining rub from the bowl.

3. Cover with clingfilm and place in the refrigerator for at least 24 hours to marinate.

4. Remove the brisket from the refrigerator for at least an hour before you want to cook it. This will allow it come back up to room temperature.

5. Prepare the barbecue for smoking and preheat to low.

6. Place the brisket on the barbecue grill, point-side up, and smoke for 10 hours with the lid on, or until the centre of the meat is no longer pink and the juices run clear.

7. Cover the beef in foil and rest in a warm place for 30 minutes before slicing and serving.

WHEN SMOKING MEATS, IT'S ALWAYS GOOD TO PLAN A FEW DAYS AHEAD AS THIS CAN BE A LENGTHY PROCESS.

Beef Rib Cutlets
with Caper & Anchovy Butter

SERVES 4

PREP: 30 MINS
+ RESTING

COOK:
20 MINS

INGREDIENTS

4 tbsp olive oil

1 tsp salt

1 tsp pepper

2 beef rib cutlets,
each weighing 800 g/
1 lb 12 oz

CAPER & ANCHOVY BUTTER

5 anchovy fillets,
chopped

200 g/7 oz butter,
softened

2 garlic cloves, crushed

40 g/1½ oz baby capers

small bunch of fresh
parsley, chopped

1 tsp salt

1 tsp pepper

1. Place the oil, salt and pepper in a non-metallic dish large enough to fit the cutlets in. Add the cutlets and turn a few times to coat thoroughly. Set aside.

2. To make the butter, place all of the ingredients into a medium bowl. Beat well with a wooden spoon until well combined.

3. Prepare the barbecue for direct cooking and preheat to medium-hot.

4. Place the cutlets on the barbecue grill and cook for 10 minutes on each side for medium rare, or to your liking. Turn every now and then and brush with the butter until the cutlets are well coated.

5. When the cutlets are cooked, cover with foil and leave in a warm place to rest for 5 minutes. Slice and serve with any remaining butter on the side.

THE CAPER & ANCHOVY BUTTER
ALSO GOES WELL
WITH ANY MEATY FISH, SUCH
AS TUNA, SALMON, SWORDFISH
OR MACKEREL.

Chuck Steak
with Black Bean Salsa

 SERVES 4 ☆

 PREP: 25 MINS

 COOK: 8 MINS

INGREDIENTS

4 tbsp olive oil

1 tsp salt

1 tsp pepper

4 chuck steaks, each
weighing 350 g/12 oz

BLACK BEAN SALSA

400 g/14 oz canned black
beans, drained

280 g/10 oz canned
sweetcorn, drained

1 small red onion, finely
chopped

1 small green pepper,
chopped

1 tbsp chipotle paste

1 tbsp soft brown sugar

small bunch of fresh
coriander, chopped

4 tbsp extra virgin
olive oil

2 tbsp sherry vinegar

1 tsp salt

1 tsp pepper

1. To make the salsa, mix together all of the ingredients in a medium bowl. Leave for 10 minutes to infuse then place in the refrigerator.

2. Prepare the barbecue for direct cooking and preheat to hot.

3. Place the oil, salt and pepper in a non-metallic dish large enough to fit the steaks in. Add the steaks and turn a few times to coat thoroughly.

4. Place the steaks on the barbecue grill and cook for 4 minutes on each side for medium-rare, or to your liking.

5. Rest the steaks in a warm place for a couple of minutes before slicing and serving with the salsa.

IF YOU LIKE YOUR STEAK
COOKED A LITTLE MORE, TRY
USING RIB-EYE INSTEAD
OF CHUCK.

Brined & Smoked
Beef Short Ribs

 SERVES 4

 PREP: 20 MINS + BRINING + RESTING

 COOK: 6 HOURS

INGREDIENTS

2 x 1 kg/2 lb 4 oz racks beef short ribs, membrane removed (ask your butcher to do this)

4 tbsp soft light brown sugar

2 tbsp old bay seasoning

BRINE

2.5 litres/4½ pints water

500 g/1 lb 2 oz sea salt crystals

250 g/9 oz brown sugar

10 cloves

20 peppercorns

small bunch of fresh thyme

3 cinnamon sticks

3 star anise

2.5 litres/4½ pints iced water

1. To make the brine, place the water, salt, sugar, cloves, peppercorns, thyme, cinnamon sticks and star anise in a large saucepan. Bring to the boil until the salt has dissolved. Turn off the heat and then add the iced water.

2. Place the ribs in a large non-metallic container and pour over the brine. Place a plate on top to keep the ribs submerged. Cover and place in the refrigerator for 24 hours. Remove the ribs from the brine for at least an hour before you want to cook them. This will allow them to come back up to room temperature.

3. Place the ribs on a board and rub in the sugar and old bay.

4. Prepare the barbecue for smoking and preheat to low. Cook, meat-side up, with a lid on for 6 hours, or until the centre of the meat is no longer pink and the juices run clear. Cover with foil and leave to rest for 30 minutes before serving.

BRINING TAKES A WHILE, SO
IT'S A GOOD IDEA TO BRINE MORE
RIBS THAN YOU NEED THEN
FREEZE THEM. THEY WILL KEEP
FOR SEVERAL MONTHS.

Rib-eye Steak
with Ranch Dressing

 SERVES 4

 PREP: 20 MINS

 COOK: 3 MINS

INGREDIENTS

4 tbsp olive oil

1 tsp salt

1 tsp pepper

4 rib-eye steaks, each weighing 280 g/10 oz

RANCH DRESSING

1 tbsp mayonnaise

1 tbsp soured cream

1 tbsp buttermilk

1 tbsp cider vinegar

1 tsp Dijon mustard

1 garlic clove, crushed

4 fresh chives, snipped

sprig of fresh parsley, chopped

sprig of fresh dill, chopped

½ tsp salt

½ tsp pepper

1. Prepare the barbecue for direct cooking and preheat to hot.

2. Place the olive oil, salt and pepper in a non-metallic dish large enough to fit all of the steaks. Add the steaks, turning them a few times to coat thoroughly.

3. To make the dressing, whisk all of the ingredients together in a small bowl. Set aside.

4. Place the steaks on the barbecue grill and cook for 4 minutes on each side for medium rare, or until cooked to your liking.

5. Rest the steaks for 2 minutes, then serve with the dressing.

ALWAYS MAKE SURE YOUR STEAKS
ARE AT ROOM TEMPERATURE BEFORE
YOU COOK THEM, AS THIS WILL HELP
THEM TO COOK MORE EVENLY.

Porterhouse Steak
in Red Wine Sauce

 SERVES 2

 PREP: 25 MINS

 COOK: 30 MINS

INGREDIENTS

2 tbsp olive oil

1 tsp salt

1 tsp pepper

2 porterhouse steaks, each weighing 350 g/ 12 oz

RED WINE SAUCE

1 tbsp olive oil

1 tbsp butter

1 red onion, finely chopped

2 garlic cloves, crushed

small bunch of fresh thyme, chopped

200 ml/7 fl oz red wine

1 tbsp flour

1 tsp Dijon mustard

1 tsp tomato purée

200 ml/7 fl oz beef stock

salt and pepper

1. Place the olive oil, salt and pepper in a non-metallic dish large enough to fit both of the steaks. Add the steaks, turning them a few times to coat thoroughly.

2. To make the red wine sauce, heat the olive oil and butter in a medium saucepan over a medium heat. Add the red onion and garlic and cook for 10 minutes, stirring every now and then until translucent and caramelized. Add the thyme and red wine and simmer until reduced by half, then add the flour, mustard and tomato purée. Slowly add the stock, stirring continually to avoid any lumps, then season with salt and pepper. When the sauce has cooked for a couple of minutes, turn off the heat and keep in a warm place.

3. Prepare the barbecue for direct cooking and preheat to hot.

4. Place the steaks on the barbecue grill and cook for 4 minutes on each side for medium rare, or cook to your liking. Leave the steaks to rest for 2 minutes in a warm place then serve with the red wine sauce.

ALWAYS TRY TO BUY AGED BEEF
AS IT HAS A MUCH BETTER
FLAVOUR AND IS MORE TENDER.

Cheddar-Jalapeño
Beef Burgers

 SERVES 4

 PREP: 20 MINS

 COOK: 10-15 MINS

INGREDIENTS

675 g/1 lb 8 oz lean
fresh beef mince

1 large egg, lightly
beaten

2 spring onions, thinly
sliced

1–2 jalapeño chillies,
deseeded and finely
chopped

2 tbsp finely chopped
fresh coriander

2 tbsp Worcestershire
sauce

½ tsp salt

½ tsp pepper

115 g/4 oz mature
Cheddar cheese, grated

TO SERVE

4 burger buns, halved
and toasted

tomato slices

lettuce

tomato ketchup

1. In a large bowl, combine the beef, egg, spring onions, chillies, coriander, Worcestershire sauce, salt and pepper. Form the mixture into eight equal-sized balls and flatten them into burgers about 1 cm/½ inch thick. Top half of the burgers with grated cheese, leaving a clear border around the edge of each burger.

2. Prepare the barbecue for direct cooking and preheat to medium-hot.

3. Place the remaining four burgers on top of the cheese-topped burgers and press the edges together to enclose the cheese. Flatten again into burgers 1–2 cm/½–¾ inch thick, making sure that the edges are well sealed.

4. Place the burgers on the barbecue grill and cook for about 5–8 minutes on each side, or until the centre of the meat is no longer pink and the juices run clear. Serve on the toasted burger buns with tomato slices, lettuce and tomato ketchup.

THE MOLTEN CHEESE CENTRE
KEEPS THESE FLAVOURSOME
BURGERS NICE AND JUICY.

Brisket Cheesesteak Subs

 SERVES 4

 PREP: 20 MINS

 COOK: 5½ HOURS

INGREDIENTS

1 kg/2 lb 4 oz beef brisket

2 tsp salt

2 tsp pepper

4 sub rolls

4 tbsp mayonnaise

FILLING

2 tbsp oil

2 tbsp butter

2 green peppers, sliced

1 onion, sliced

1 tsp salt

1 tsp pepper

600 g/1 lb 5 oz pizza mozzarella, grated

1. Prepare the barbecue for indirect cooking and preheat to medium-low.

2. Put the beef on a board and gently rub in the salt and pepper.

3. Place the beef point-side up on the barbecue grill and cook for 5 hours with the lid on. Check that the beef is cooked through and the juices run clear. Remove from the barbecue and leave to cool completely.

4. To make the filling, heat the oil and butter in a frying pan and cook the peppers and onion over a medium heat for 10 minutes, or until the vegetables are soft to the touch. Sprinkle with the salt and pepper.

5. Preheat a grill to high. Slice the beef as thinly as possible and divide into four piles on a baking tray. Top each beef pile with the peppers, onions and grated cheese. Grill until all of the cheese has melted.

6. Cut the sub rolls in half lengthways, spread with the mayonnaise and then fill with piles of the beef mixture. Serve immediately.

CAN'T FIND SUB ROLLS?
TRY USING SMALL FRENCH
STICKS OR A LARGE FRENCH
STICK CUT INTO FOUR.

Beef Sausages
with Scorched Tomato Relish

 SERVES 4

 PREP: 30 MINS + CHILLING

 COOK: 35-40 MINS

INGREDIENTS

SAUSAGES

1 kg/2 lb 2 oz beef chuck, diced and chilled

100 g/3½ oz beef suet

2 tsp fennel seeds

2 tsp dried thyme

small bunch of fresh parsley, chopped

1 tbsp Dijon mustard

2 tsp salt

1 tsp pepper

1 tbsp tomato purée

105 cm/42 inch sausage casing

SCORCHED TOMATO RELISH

4 tbsp olive oil

2 tbsp red wine vinegar

1 tbsp sugar

4 large tomatoes, halved

1 red pepper, halved and stalk removed

1 red onion, quartered

1 large red chilli

4 garlic cloves

handful of fresh parsley

1 tsp salt

1 tsp pepper

1. To make the sausages, mix the diced beef with the suet, fennel seeds, thyme, parsley, mustard, salt, pepper and tomato purée in a large bowl.

2. Using a mincer, mince the beef mixture using the course mincing plate. Refrigerate the minced meat for 30 minutes.

3. Soak the sausage casing according to the package instructions. Thread the casing onto a sausage stuffer and tie off the end. Fill the sausage stuffer with the chilled filling.

4. Hold the casing steady and fill with the filling. When the casing is filled, lay the sausage down in a straight line and prick all the way along with a pin. Turn over and repeat on the other side. Twist and snip into four long sausages.

5. Prepare the barbecue for direct cooking and preheat to medium-hot.

6. To make the relish, mix all the ingredients in a large bowl, then tip into a baking tray. Place on the barbecue grill and cook with the lid on for 25 minutes, or until all the vegetables are slightly charred and softened. Leave to cool slightly.

7. Tip all of the cooled vegetables onto a chopping board and chop with a knife into a rough relish. Place the sausages on the barbecue grill for 6 minutes on each side, or until the centre of the sausage is no longer pink and the juices run clear. Serve the sausages immediately with the relish.

TRY USING HEIRLOOM TOMATOES AND POBLANO CHILLIES FOR A MORE UNUSUAL RELISH.

Chapter 3
PORK & LAMB

Pulled Pork
with Sweet Potato Mash

 ☆ SERVES 6-8 ☆

 PREP: 20 MINS + RESTING

 COOK: 12¼ HOURS

INGREDIENTS

3 kg/6 lb 8 oz pork shoulder, skin removed and bone in

RUB

1 tbsp paprika

2 tbsp light brown sugar

1 tsp dried thyme

1 tsp dried oregano

2 tsp pepper

1 tsp garlic salt

1 tsp celery salt

1 tsp salt

1 tsp onion powder

CHILLI SAUCE

2 tbsp yellow American-style mustard

2 tbsp cider vinegar

2 tbsp treacle

2 tbsp tomato ketchup

1 tbsp sriracha chilli sauce

SWEET POTATO MASH

1 kg/2 lb 4 oz sweet potatoes, diced

200 g/7 oz salted butter, diced

1 tsp pepper

1. Prepare the barbecue for smoking and preheat to low.

2. Combine all of the rub ingredients together in a small bowl.

3. Place the pork on a chopping board and massage the rub all over the pork.

4. Place the pork on the barbecue grill, making sure the pork is fat-side up. Close the lid and cook for 12 hours, or until a thick dark golden crust has formed. Check that the centre of the meat is no longer pink and that the juices run clear. Cover in foil and leave to rest in a warm place for 30 minutes.

5. Mix together the mustard, vinegar, treacle, ketchup and chilli sauce in a small bowl. Set aside.

6. Boil or steam the sweet potatoes in a large saucepan until soft when pricked with a knife. Drain and mash, then beat in the butter and pepper.

7. Remove any bones from the pork and pull the meat into large chunks. The meat should be very tender, so this should not be hard to do. Put the pork in a large bowl and tip over the chilli sauce. Gently mix, trying not to break the pork up too much.

8. Serve the pork with the sweet potato mash.

IT'S PROBABLY BEST TO COOK
YOUR PORK FROM EARLY IN THE
MORNING TO AVOID HAVING TO
EAT VERY LATE.

Spicy Baby Back Ribs

SERVES 4

PREP: 20 MINS + MARINATING

COOK: 4 HOURS

INGREDIENTS

4 racks baby back pork
ribs, each weighing
500 g/1 lb 2 oz

SPICY MARINADE

2 tbsp soft brown sugar

3 tbsp old bay seasoning

1 tbsp Worcestershire
sauce

4 tsp salt

APPLE GLAZE

150 ml/5 fl oz apple
juice

2 tbsp olive oil

2 tbsp cider vinegar

1. To make the spicy marinade, mix together all the ingredients in a large bowl then add the pork ribs and turn to coat thoroughly.

2. Lay the ribs in a non-metallic dish, adding any remaining marinade from the bowl. Cover the dish with clingfilm and place in the refrigerator for at least 12 hours to marinate.

3. Remove the ribs from the refrigerator for at least an hour before you want to cook them. This will allow them to come back up to room temperature.

4. To make the apple glaze, mix together the apple juice, olive oil and cider vinegar in a small bowl and set aside.

5. Prepare the barbecue for indirect cooking and preheat to medium-low.

6. Cook the ribs on the barbecue grill for 4 hours, with the lid on. Brush the ribs on each side with the apple glaze every 30 minutes.

7. When the ribs are cooked through and the meat is falling off the bone, remove from the barbecue. Check that the centre of the meat is no longer pink and the juices run clear, then serve immediately.

PORK RIBS TEND TO GET STUCK IN YOUR TEETH SO IT'S ALWAYS GOOD TO HAVE SOME TOOTHPICKS TO HAND.

Braised Pork Belly
with Apple & Mustard Ketchup

SERVES 4

PREP: 25 MINS + RESTING

COOK: 2¼ HOURS

INGREDIENTS

small bunch of fresh thyme

1 bulb of fennel, sliced

1 onion, sliced

1.5 kg/3 lb 5 oz pork belly

575 ml/18 fl oz dry cider

300 ml/10 fl oz chicken stock

150 ml/5 fl oz cider vinegar

55 g/2 oz honey

1 tsp salt

1 tsp pepper

APPLE & MUSTARD KETCHUP

juice of 2 lemons

55 g/2 oz sugar

3 cooking apples, peeled, cored and chopped

2 tbsp American-style yellow mustard

1. Prepare the barbecue for indirect cooking and preheat to medium.

2. Place the thyme, fennel and onion in a deep baking tray slightly bigger than the pork. Place the pork belly on top.

3. In a medium bowl, mix together the cider, stock, vinegar and honey.

4. Pour the cider mixture over the pork and then sprinkle over salt and pepper.

5. Place the baking tray on the barbecue grill and cover the barbecue with the lid. Cook for 2 hours, or until the pork meat is soft to the touch and a crackling has formed. Check that the centre of the meat is no longer pink and the juices run clear.

6. Place all of the ketchup ingredients in a medium microwave-proof bowl. Cover with microwaveable clingfilm and cook on high for 4 minutes, or until the apples start to fall apart. Blend the ketchup with a hand blender until smooth and leave to cool down.

7. When the pork is cooked, remove the pork from the barbecue and leave in a warm place to rest for 30 minutes. Strain the juices from the baking tray into a medium saucepan and simmer until the liquid is reduced by half.

8. Serve the pork with the cooking juices poured over the top and the ketchup on the side.

FOR THE ULTIMATE
SANDWICH, JUST CUT THE PORK
INTO SLICES AND ADD
BREAD AND COLESLAW!

Pork Belly Sliders
with Kimchi Slaw

☆ MAKES 14 ☆

PREP: 20 MINS + COOLING

COOK: 2¼ HOURS

INGREDIENTS

1 kg/2 lb 4 oz pork belly

3 star anise

1 cinnamon stick

5 dried shiitake mushrooms

5 spring onions

200 g/7 oz sugar

100 ml/3½ fl oz light soy sauce

300 ml/10 fl oz rice wine

100 ml/3½ fl oz rice vinegar

14 burger or slider buns

6 tbsp Japanese mayonnaise, for spreading

KIMCHI SLAW

3 tbsp Japanese mayonnaise

½ Chinese cabbage, shredded

200 g/7 oz kimchi, sliced

4 spring onions, sliced

20 g/¾ oz pickled ginger, chopped

1. Preheat the oven to 180°C/350°F/Gas Mark 4.

2. Place the pork belly, star anise, cinnamon stick, mushrooms, spring onions, sugar, soy sauce, rice wine and rice vinegar in a baking dish. Cover with greaseproof paper and foil.

3. Roast in the preheated oven for 2 hours, or until the centre of the meat is no longer pink and the juices run clear. Leave to cool completely in the cooking liquor.

4. To make the slaw, mix together all the ingredients in a medium bowl.

5. Prepare the barbecue for direct cooking and preheat to medium-hot.

6. Slice the pork into 2 cm/¾ inch thick slices. Place the slices on the barbecue grill and cook for 3—4 minutes on each side, or until starting to caramelize.

7. Cut the pork slices into squares. Cut the buns in half, spread with mayonnaise then fill with the pork and slaw.

ANY LEFTOVER PORK BELLY
FROM THIS RECIPE CAN ALSO
BE USED IN STIR-FRIES OR
NOODLE SOUPS.

Chilli Hot Dogs
with Texan Chilli

 SERVES 4

 PREP: 20 MINS

 COOK: 2½ HOURS

INGREDIENTS

TEXAN CHILLI

4 tbsp olive oil

1 onion, diced

1 celery stick, diced

2 garlic cloves, crushed

350 g/12 oz minced beef

1 tbsp flour

1 tbsp paprika

1 tbsp ground cumin

1 tbsp ground coriander

1 tsp dried oregano

1 tsp onion powder

1 tsp chilli powder

1 tsp dried thyme

400 ml/14 fl oz passata

400 ml/14 fl oz beef stock

salt and pepper

HOT DOGS

4 large hot dog sausages

4 hot dog rolls

yellow American-style mustard, to serve

1 onion, chopped

1. To make the chilli, heat the oil in a medium saucepan and sweat the onion, celery and garlic over a low heat. Cook with a lid on for 10 minutes, or until the vegetables are translucent and softened.

2. Turn up the heat a little and add the beef. Cook for another 10 minutes, breaking up the mince with a wooden spoon.

3. Add the flour, paprika, cumin, coriander, oregano, onion powder, chilli powder and thyme, stirring a few times. Slowly add the passata and beef stock. Season with salt and pepper and cook over a low heat with a lid on for 2 hours, or until the meat is tender and the sauce has thickened. Turn off the heat and leave in a warm place.

4. Prepare the barbecue for direct cooking and preheat to medium-hot.

5. Place the hot dogs on the barbecue grill and cook for 10 minutes, turning every now and then. Check that the sausages are cooked through and the centre of the meat is no longer pink.

6. Serve the hot dogs in the rolls, topped with the chilli, mustard and chopped onion.

THIS CHILLI CAN BE MADE THE DAY BEFORE; IT'S ALSO GREAT WITH BURGERS FOR A SLOPPY JOE.

Italian Sausage Subs
with Peppers & Onions

 SERVES 4

 PREP: 40 MINS + CHILLING

 COOK: 20-25 MINS

INGREDIENTS

ITALIAN SAUSAGES

1 kg/2 lb 4 oz diced
pork shoulder, chilled

2 tsp fennel seeds

2 tsp dried sage

2 tsp dried thyme

bunch of chopped parsley

zest of 2 lemons

2 tsp salt

1 tsp pepper

1 tsp chilli flakes

105 cm/42 inch sausage
casing

oil, for brushing

FILLING

4 tbsp olive oil

1 red pepper, diced

1 yellow pepper, diced

1 red onion, diced

2 tbsp red wine vinegar

1 tsp salt

1 tsp pepper

4 sub rolls

6 tbsp mayonnaise

handful of rocket

1. To make the sausages, mix the pork shoulder with all the other ingredients in a large bowl until the pork is coated thoroughly.

2. Using a mincer, mince the pork and other sausage ingredients using a course mincing plate. Refrigerate the minced meat for 30 minutes.

3. Soak the sausage casing according to the package instructions. Thread the casing onto a sausage stuffer and tie off the end. Fill the sausage stuffer with the chilled filling.

4. Hold the casing steady and fill with the filling. When the casing is filled, lay the sausage down in a straight line and prick all the way along with a pin. Turn over and repeat on the other side. Twist and snip into four long sausages.

5. To make the filling, heat the oil in a medium frying pan. Add the peppers and onion and cook on a medium heat for 10 minutes, or until the peppers and onions are softened. Add the vinegar, salt and pepper then turn off the heat.

6. Prepare the barbecue for direct cooking and preheat to medium-hot. Lightly brush the barbecue grill with oil and cook the sausages for 6 minutes on each side, or until the centre of the meat is no longer pink and the juices run clear.

7. Cut the sub rolls down the middle, fill each with mayonnaise, one of the sausages and the pepper mixture. Finish with a little rocket and serve.

Pork Meatball Skewers
with Smoked Cheese Sauce

 ☆ SERVES 4 ☆

 PREP: 30 MINS

 COOK: 20-25 MINS

INGREDIENTS

450 g/1 lb pork mince

2 tbsp olive oil, plus extra for brushing

2 shallots, finely chopped

100 g/3½ oz panko breadcrumbs

100 ml/3½ fl oz milk

1 tsp fennel seeds

1 tsp dried oregano

1 large egg, beaten

55 g/2 oz grated Parmesan cheese, plus extra to serve

1 tsp salt

1 tsp pepper

4 large gherkins, sliced

SMOKED CHEESE SAUCE

55 g/2 oz butter

40 g/1½ oz flour

600 ml/1 pint whole milk

1 tbsp yellow American-style mustard

150 g/5½ oz smoked cheese, grated

½ tsp salt

½ tsp pepper

1. To make the meatballs, place the pork mince, oil, shallots, breadcrumbs, milk, fennel seeds, oregano, beaten egg, Parmesan, salt and pepper in a large bowl and mix well to combine. Divide the mixture into golf-ball-sized balls. Place the balls on four metal skewers.

2. Prepare the barbecue for direct cooking and preheat to medium-hot.

3. Meanwhile, make the cheese sauce by melting the butter on a low heat in a medium saucepan. Add the flour and cook until a light golden colour.

4. In a small saucepan, bring the milk to the boil and then add it slowly to the butter mixture, stirring continuously with a wooden spoon to avoid any lumps. When all the milk has been added, add the mustard, cheese, salt and pepper. Remove from the heat and set aside in a warm place.

5. Lightly brush the barbecue grill with oil and cook the skewers with the lid on for 10—12 minutes, turning every now and then. When the skewers are cooked through and the juices run clear, remove from the barbecue and serve with the cheese sauce, sliced gherkins and Parmesan.

IF YOU DON'T LIKE SMOKED CHEESE, THIS RECIPE WILL ALSO WORK WITH CHEDDAR OR ANY BLUE CHEESE.

Lamb Burgers
with Tzatziki & Feta

☆ SERVES 4 ☆

PREP: 15 MINS

COOK: 10 MINS

INGREDIENTS

BURGERS

500 g/1 lb 2 oz minced lamb

1 tsp salt

1 tsp pepper

1 tsp cumin seeds

TZATZIKI

4 tbsp Greek yogurt

small bunch of fresh mint, chopped

small bunch of fresh dill, chopped

½ cucumber, sliced

½ tsp salt

½ tsp pepper

PICKLED ONION

1 red onion, sliced

2 tbsp red wine vinegar

½ tsp salt

oil, for brushing

4 burger buns

100 g/3½ oz feta, crumbled

1. To make the burgers, mix the lamb, salt, pepper and cumin seeds together in a medium bowl.

2. Divide the mince mixture into four equal balls then shape into patties.

3. To make the tzatziki, mix all of the ingredients in a small bowl and stir to combine.

4. To make the pickled onion, mix together the onion, vinegar and salt in another small bowl.

5. Prepare the barbecue for direct cooking and preheat to medium-hot.

6. Brush the barbecue grill with a little oil. Cook the burgers for 5 minutes on each side, or until the centre of the meat is no longer pink and the juices run clear.

7. Divide the burgers between the buns and top with the tzatziki, feta and pickled onions. Serve immediately.

THESE LAMB BURGERS MAKE
A GREAT ALTERNATIVE TO
TRADITIONAL BEEF OR CHICKEN
BURGERS.

Lamb Kebabs

☆ SERVES 4 ☆

PREP: 20 MINS

COOK: 10 MINS

INGREDIENTS

LAMB SKEWERS

1 kg/2 lb 4 oz lamb neck fillets, diced

2 tbsp olive oil

1 tsp paprika

1 tsp dried oregano

1 tsp ground cumin

1 tsp dried thyme

1 tsp salt

1 tsp pepper

4 large flat breads

4 tbsp Greek yogurt

1 large tomato, chopped

1 small red onion, sliced

100 g/3½ oz red cabbage, shredded

small bunch of fresh coriander, chopped

2 lemons, halved

sriracha or other hot chilli sauce

1. To make the lamb skewers, mix the lamb, oil, paprika, oregano, cumin, thyme, salt and pepper in a medium bowl and stir to coat the lamb thoroughly.

2. Prepare the barbecue for direct cooking and preheat to hot.

3. Thread the lamb onto four metal skewers. Place on the barbecue grill and cook on all four sides for 2 minutes for medium-rare, or to your liking. Check that the centre of the meat is no longer pink and the juices run clear. Leave the lamb to rest for a couple of minutes in a warm place.

4. Place the flat breads on the barbecue grill and cook on both sides until pliable. This should only take a few seconds.

5. Remove the lamb from the skewers. Spread the flat breads with the yogurt and top with lamb pieces, tomato, onion, cabbage and coriander. Squeeze the lemons over the top and drizzle with chilli sauce.

NAAN BREADS ARE A GREAT
ALTERNATIVE TO FLAT BREADS.
THEY WILL NEED JUST
A FEW SECONDS MORE TO
HEAT THROUGH.

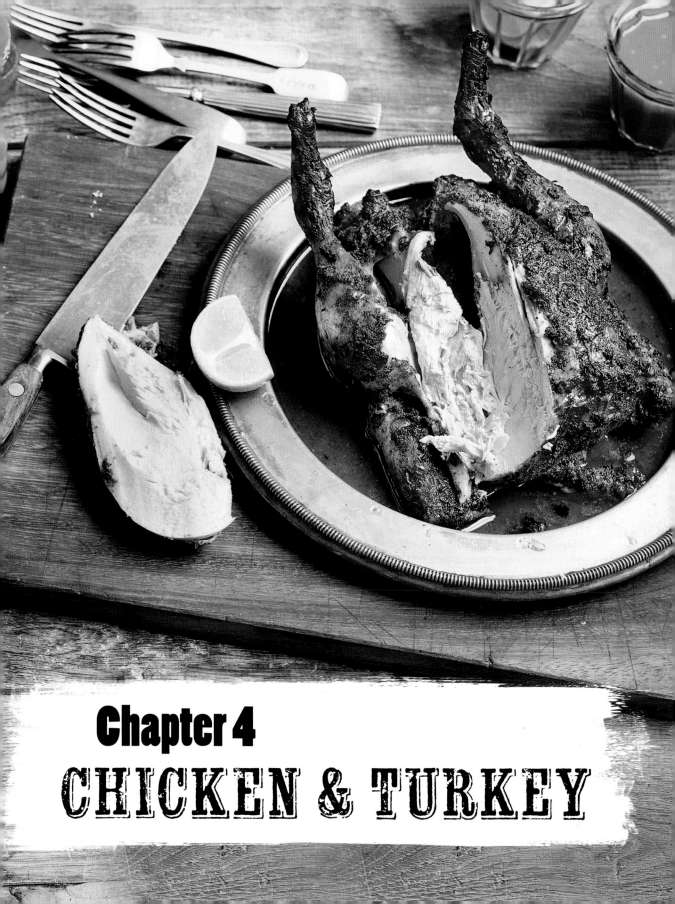

Chapter 4
CHICKEN & TURKEY

Sticky Bourbon
Chicken Wings

 ☆ SERVES 4 ☆

PREP: 20 MINS

COOK: 30 MINS

INGREDIENTS

1 kg/2 lb 4 oz chicken wings, tips removed

oil, for brushing

RUB

1 tbsp paprika

½ tsp ground cumin

1 tsp dried thyme

1 tsp dried oregano

1 tsp salt

1 tsp pepper

BOURBON GLAZE

2 tbsp bourbon

2 tbsp cider vinegar

1 tbsp Worcestershire sauce

2 tbsp treacle

2 tbsp tomato ketchup

2 tbsp chipotle paste

1 tbsp American-style yellow mustard

½ tsp salt

½ tsp pepper

1. To make the rub, combine all of the ingredients together in a large bowl.

2. Cut each chicken wing in half. Add the wing pieces to the bowl containing the rub and turn until coated thoroughly.

3. To make the bourbon glaze, place a medium saucepan over a medium heat. Add the bourbon and flambé. When the flames have gone, add the rest of the glaze ingredients and simmer over a medium heat until the sauce has reduced by half.

4. Prepare the barbecue for direct cooking and preheat to medium-hot.

5. Thread half of the chicken wing pieces onto two metal skewers, creating a raft shape. Repeat with the other half of the wings. Brush the wings with the bourbon glaze.

6. Brush the barbecue grill lightly with oil and cook the wings for 10 minutes on each side, brushing with more glaze as they cook.

7. When the wings are cooked, the meat should come easily away from the bone. Check that the juices run clear when the thickest part of the meat is pierced with a skewer and the centre of the meat is no longer pink. Remove from the skewers and serve.

TRY MAKING A LARGER BATCH OF
THE BOURBON GLAZE AS IT WILL
KEEP IN THE REFRIGERATOR FOR AT
LEAST A MONTH AND CAN BE USED
AS A CONDIMENT.

BBQ Chicken Wings

INGREDIENTS

1 kg/2 lb 4 oz chicken
wings, tips removed

oil, for brushing

BBQ MARINADE

1 tbsp paprika

2 tbsp olive oil

2 tbsp tomato ketchup

2 tbsp American-style
yellow mustard

2 tbsp maple syrup

1 tbsp Worcestershire
sauce

1. To make the marinade, mix together all the ingredients in a large bowl. Add the chicken wings and use your hands to mix and coat thoroughly in the marinade.

2. Cover the bowl with clingfilm and place in the refrigerator for at least 2 hours.

3. Remove the chicken wings from the refrigerator for at least an hour before you want to cook them. This will allow them to come back up to room temperature.

4. Prepare the barbecue for direct cooking and preheat to medium-hot.

5. Lightly brush the barbecue grill with oil. Cook the chicken wings for 10 minutes on both sides, or until they are caramelized, slightly charred and the meat comes easily away from the bone. Check that the juices run clear when the thickest part of the meat is pierced with a skewer and the centre of the meat is no longer pink, then serve immediately.

CHICKEN WING TIPS CAN
BE SAVED AND USED TO
MAKE STOCK.

Chicken Drumsticks
with Satay Glaze

 SERVES 4

 PREP: 20 MINS + MARINATING

 COOK: 25 MINS

INGREDIENTS

1 kg/2 lb 4 oz chicken drumsticks

SOY MARINADE

2 tbsp light soy sauce

2 tbsp soft light brown sugar

1 tsp turmeric

1 tbsp sesame oil

1 tbsp vegetable oil

SATAY GLAZE

150 ml/5 fl oz coconut cream

2 tbsp peanut butter

1 tbsp sriracha chilli sauce

2 tbsp soft light brown sugar

1 tsp fish sauce

1. To make the marinade, place all of the marinade ingredients into a non-metallic dish big enough to fit the chicken in. Add the chicken, turning a few times to coat thoroughly. Cover with clingfilm and place in the refrigerator for at least 2 hours.

2. Remove the chicken from the refrigerator for at least an hour before you want to cook it. This will allow it to come back up to room temperature.

3. To make the satay glaze, place all of the ingredients in a small saucepan and stir with a wooden spoon until well combined. Cook for 5 minutes, or until slightly syrupy.

4. Prepare the barbecue for direct cooking and preheat to medium.

5. Place the chicken on the barbecue grill and cook the drumsticks for 20 minutes, turning every now and then and basting with the satay glaze.

6. Check the chicken is cooked by seeing that the juices run clear when the thickest part of the meat is pierced with a skewer and the centre of the meat is no longer pink. Glaze one last time and serve.

IF YOU HAVE ANY OF THE GLAZE
LEFT OVER, IT'S GREAT IN A
NOODLE SALAD, WITH PRAWNS,
CHICKEN AND BASIL.

Ancho Chilli, Vanilla
& Cola Chicken

 SERVES 4

 PREP: 20 MINS + MARINATING

 COOK: 45 MINS

INGREDIENTS

4 chicken supremes, skin on

PAPRIKA MARINADE

4 tbsp olive oil

1 tsp dried thyme

1 tbsp paprika

1 tbsp soft brown sugar

1 tbsp ground cumin

1 tsp salt

1 tsp pepper

ANCHO CHILLI SAUCE

2 dried ancho chillies, roughly chopped and stalks removed

1 tsp dried oregano

330 ml/10½ fl oz cola

155 g/5½ oz treacle

1 tsp vanilla extract

400 g/14 oz canned plum tomatoes

150 ml/5 fl oz cider vinegar

1. To make the marinade, place all of the marinade ingredients into a non-metallic dish big enough to fit the chicken in. Add the chicken, turning a few times to coat thoroughly. Cover with clingfilm and place in the refrigerator for at least 2 hours.

2. Remove the chicken from the refrigerator for at least an hour before you want to cook it. This will allow it to come back up to room temperature.

3. To make the sauce, place all of the sauce ingredients in a medium saucepan and cook over a low heat for 30 minutes, or until the sauce has reduced by half. Stir every now and then.

4. When the sauce is ready, remove from the heat and leave to cool slightly. Blend thoroughly with a hand blender.

5. Prepare the barbecue for direct cooking and preheat to medium-hot.

6. Place the chicken skin-side down on the barbecue grill for 6 minutes, then turn over and cook for another 6 minutes. Check the chicken is cooked by seeing that the juices run clear when the thickest part of the meat is pierced with a skewer and the centre of the meat is no longer pink. Leave the chicken in a warm place for a couple of minutes before serving with the sauce.

FOR A SUPER SPICY SAUCE,
TRY ADDING A FEW HABANERO
CHILLIES AS WELL.

Honey & Orange
Turkey Breast

 SERVES 4

 PREP: 30 MINS
+ BRINING
+ RESTING

 COOK: 6 HOURS

INGREDIENTS

3 kg/6 lb 8 oz turkey crown, skin on

BRINE

2.5 litres/4½ pints water

500 g/1 lb 2 oz sea salt crystals

250 g/9 oz honey

zest and juice of 3 oranges

10 cloves

20 peppercorns

small bunch of fresh thyme, chopped

3 cinnamon sticks

2.5 litres/4½ pints cranberry juice

1. To make the brine, place 575 ml/18 fl oz of the water in a large saucepan. Add the salt, honey, orange zest, orange juice, cloves, peppercorns, thyme and cinnamon sticks. Bring to the boil until the salt has dissolved. Turn off the heat and then add the rest of the water. Add the cranberry juice and leave to cool completely.

2. Place the turkey crown in a large non-metallic container and pour over the brine. Place a plate on top to keep the turkey submerged. Cover and put in the refrigerator overnight.

3. Remove the turkey from the refrigerator for at least an hour before you want to cook it. This will allow it to come back up to room temperature.

4. Prepare the barbecue for smoking and preheat to low.

5. Place the turkey, skin-side up, on the barbecue grill and cook with a lid on for 6 hours. Check the turkey is cooked by seeing that the juices run clear when the thickest part of the meat is pierced with a skewer and the centre of the meat is no longer pink. Cover with foil and leave to rest for 30 minutes in a warm place before slicing and serving.

THIS SMOKED TURKEY TASTES GREAT ON ITS OWN AND IT ALSO MAKES AN AWESOME ADDITION TO A SANDWICH OR SALAD.

Turkey Drumsticks
with Mexican Spice Rub

SERVES 4

PREP: 20 MINS
+ MARINATING
+ RESTING

COOK:
40 MINS

INGREDIENTS

4 turkey drumsticks,
each weighing 500 g/
1 lb 2 oz

MEXICAN RUB

2 tbsp soft brown sugar

2 tbsp olive oil

zest and juice of
1 orange

1 tbsp salt

1 tbsp paprika

1 tsp pepper

1 tsp garlic salt

1 tbsp chipotle purée

1 tbsp ground cumin

1 tsp dried oregano

1 tsp dried thyme

1. To make the rub, mix all of the ingredients together in a large bowl. Add the turkey drumsticks, turning a few times to coat thoroughly.

2. Cover with clingfilm and place in the refrigerator for at least 2 hours. Remove the drumsticks from the refrigerator for at least an hour before you want to cook them. This will allow them to come back up to room temperature.

3. Prepare the barbecue for indirect cooking and preheat to medium.

4. Place the turkey on the barbecue grill and cook for 40 minutes with the lid on. Check the turkey is cooked by seeing that the juices run clear when the thickest part of the meat is pierced with a skewer and the centre of the meat is no longer pink.

5. Cover with foil and leave to rest in a warm place before serving.

WET RUBS CAN BE MADE WELL IN ADVANCE AND KEPT IN A JAR IN THE REFRIGERATOR FOR UP TO TWO WEEKS.

Teriyaki Chicken Skewers

SERVES 4

PREP: 20 MINS + MARINATING

COOK: 20 MINS

INGREDIENTS

500 g/1 lb 2 oz
skinless, boneless
chicken thighs

2 tbsp light soy sauce

1 tbsp sesame oil

1 tbsp vegetable oil,
plus extra for brushing

1 bunch of spring
onions, cut into 5-cm/
2-inch pieces

TERIYAKI SAUCE

2 tbsp light soy sauce

2 tbsp mirin

1 tbsp rice vinegar

2.5-cm/1-inch piece of
fresh ginger, sliced

55 g/2 oz sugar

1. Cut the chicken into bite-sized pieces and place in a non-metallic bowl. Add the soy sauce and the oils and mix until the pieces are coated thoroughly.

2. Cover the bowl with clingfilm and place in the refrigerator for at least 2 hours. Remove the chicken from the refrigerator for at least an hour before you want to cook it. This will allow it to come back up to room temperature.

3. To make the sauce, heat all of the ingredients in a small saucepan over a medium heat until it is reduced by half and slightly syrupy. Remove from the heat and discard the ginger.

4. Prepare the barbecue for direct cooking and preheat to medium-hot.

5. Place the chicken pieces and spring onions onto four metal skewers.

6. Lightly brush the barbecue grill with oil and cook the skewers for 5 minutes on each side. Brush the chicken skewers with the teriyaki sauce while cooking.

7. Check the chicken is cooked and the centre of the meat is no longer pink. Brush the chicken pieces and spring onions with the sauce one last time and serve.

ALWAYS WASH THE SPRING
ONIONS BEFORE USE TO REMOVE
ANY GRIT OR DIRT.

Bacon-wrapped Chicken
Burger with Grilled Pineapple

SERVES 4

PREP: 20 MINS

COOK: 25 MINS

INGREDIENTS

8 smoked pancetta rashers

4 skinless, boneless chicken breasts

oil, for brushing

1 baby gem lettuce, shredded

4 burger buns

GRILLED PINEAPPLE

½ a medium pineapple

1 tbsp demerara sugar

1 tsp pepper

RUSSIAN DRESSING

3 tbsp mayonnaise

1 tbsp tomato ketchup

1 tbsp horseradish

2 tsp hot pepper sauce

1 tbsp Worcestershire sauce

1 shallot, grated

1. Lay two slices of the pancetta rashers next to each other on a chopping board. Place a chicken breast on top of the rashers and wrap the rashers all the way around the breast. Repeat with the other three breasts.

2. To make the grilled pineapple, peel the pineapple and cut into four thick rings. Remove the core then sprinkle each ring on both sides with the sugar and pepper.

3. Prepare the barbecue for direct cooking and preheat to medium-hot.

4. To make the dressing, mix all the ingredients together in a bowl then set aside.

5. Brush your barbecue grill with oil, then place the chicken breasts on the grill. Cook for 10 minutes on each side, or until the juices run clear when the thickest part of the meat is pierced with a skewer and the centre of the meat is no longer pink. When the chicken is cooked, remove from the heat and leave in a warm place to rest for 4 minutes.

6. While you are waiting for the chicken to rest, grill the pineapple rings for 2 minutes on each side, or until caramelized.

7. Divide the chicken, pineapple rings, lettuce and dressing between the burger buns and serve immediately.

THIS BURGER IS A REAL MIX OF GORGEOUS FLAVOURS, WITH THE CHICKEN, BACON, PINEAPPLE AND DRESSING ALL PACKING A PUNCH.

Chapter 5
FISH & SEAFOOD

Whole Grilled Prawns
in Maple & Sriracha Butter

 SERVES 4 PREP: 15 MINS COOK: 10-15 MINS

INGREDIENTS

1 kg/2 lb 4 oz whole large raw prawns

MAPLE & SRIRACHA BUTTER

150 g/5½ oz butter

2 tbsp maple syrup

2 tbsp sriracha chilli sauce

1 tbsp cider vinegar

½ tsp salt

½ tsp pepper

1. Prepare the barbecue for direct cooking and preheat to hot.

2. Thread half of the prawns onto two metal skewers, creating a raft shape. This will make cooking the prawns a lot easier. Repeat with the other half of the prawns.

3. To make the butter, melt the butter in a small saucepan over a low heat. Add the maple syrup, chilli sauce, vinegar, salt and pepper and stir to combine. Remove from the heat and keep in a warm place.

4. Place the prawns on the barbecue grill and cook for 3 minutes on both sides, or until cooked through and the shells have turned dark pink.

5. Once the prawns are cooked, remove the skewers. Place the prawns in a medium bowl and pour over the butter. Mix well and serve immediately.

IF USING WOODEN SKEWERS, MAKE SURE YOU SOAK THEM FIRST TO STOP THEM BURNING.

Scallops
with Hot Soy Sauce

 SERVES 2

 PREP: 20 MINS

 COOK: 15 MINS

INGREDIENTS

12 large fresh scallops,
cleaned and roes removed

1 tsp salt

1 tsp pepper

oil, for brushing

HOT SOY SAUCE

1 tbsp oil

1 tbsp sesame oil

1 garlic clove, chopped

2 tbsp rice wine

2 tbsp light soy sauce

1 tbsp sugar

1 tbsp oyster sauce

2.5-cm/1-inch piece of
fresh ginger, cut into
matchsticks

4 spring onions, sliced

1 red bird's eye chilli,
sliced

1. To make the soy sauce, heat the oils in a small saucepan over a medium heat. Add the garlic and cook for 30 seconds, then add the rice wine, soy sauce, sugar and oyster sauce. Reduce by half then add the ginger, spring onions and chilli. Remove from the heat and set aside.

2. Prepare the barbecue for direct cooking and preheat to hot.

3. Thread the scallops onto four metal skewers and sprinkle the skewers with the salt and pepper.

4. Brush the barbecue grill with a little oil. Cook the scallops for 30 seconds on each side, or until the scallops are caramelized on the outside, but still creamy in the middle.

5. Remove from the skewers and serve with the hot soy sauce.

WHENEVER POSSIBLE, BUY
HAND-DIVED SCALLOPS AS THIS
METHOD HAS MUCH LESS OF AN
ENVIRONMENTAL IMPACT.

Peppered Tuna Steaks
with Anchovy Mayo

 SERVES 4

 PREP: 25 MINS

 COOK: 2 MINS

INGREDIENTS

4 tbsp olive oil

1 tsp salt

1 tsp pepper

4 tuna steaks, each weighing 250 g/9 oz

lemon wedges, to serve

ANCHOVY MAYO

1 egg yolk

splash of water

4 anchovy fillets

1 garlic clove, crushed

2 tsp Dijon mustard

200 ml/7 fl oz rapeseed oil

1 tbsp white wine vinegar

salt and pepper

1. To make the mayo, place the egg yolk, water, anchovy fillets, garlic and Dijon mustard in a food processor and blitz for 30 seconds, or until everything has doubled in volume. With the motor still running, start to add the oil very slowly. When all of the oil has been added and the mayonnaise has thickened, season with salt and pepper and then add the vinegar. Transfer the mayo to a small bowl.

2. Prepare the barbecue for direct cooking and preheat to hot.

3. Place the olive oil, salt and pepper in a non-metallic dish large enough to hold all of the tuna steaks. Add the tuna, turning a few times to coat thoroughly.

4. Place the tuna on the barbecue grill and cook for 1 minute on each side for rare, or to your liking. Serve with the mayo and lemon wedges.

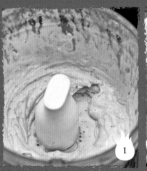

HOME-MADE MAYONNAISE IS AMAZING BUT, IF YOU REALLY DON'T HAVE THE TIME, SHOP BOUGHT WILL DO JUST FINE.

Grilled Trout Tacos

 SERVES 2

 PREP: 20 MINS

 COOK: 12 MINS

INGREDIENTS

1 small red onion,
sliced into rings

1 red jalapeño chilli,
sliced

2 tbsp red wine vinegar

½ tsp salt

2 whole trout, gutted
and cleaned, each
weighing 375 g–400 g/
13 oz–14 oz

2 tbsp olive oil

1 tsp dried oregano

1 tsp cumin seeds

1 tsp paprika

½ tsp salt

½ tsp pepper

6 soft tacos or small
tortillas

FILLINGS

1 ripe avocado, chopped

juice of ½ lime

2 tbsp soured cream

55 g/2 oz salted
ricotta, grated

small bunch of fresh
coriander, finely chopped

lime wedges, to serve

1. Place the onion, chilli, vinegar and salt in a small bowl. Mix together with a spoon and then leave to pickle slightly.

2. Score the trout on both sides; this will help speed up the cooking process.

3. In a shallow non-metallic dish large enough to hold the trout, mix together the oil, oregano, cumin seeds, paprika, salt and pepper. Then add the trout, turning a couple of times to coat thoroughly.

4. Start to prepare the fillings by placing the avocado in a small bowl. Squeeze over the lime juice and set aside.

5. Prepare the barbecue for direct cooking and preheat to medium-hot.

6. Place the trout on the barbecue grill and cook for 5 minutes on both sides, or until the flesh comes easily away from the bone. Check that the fish is opaque and flaky when separated with a fork.

7. Leave the trout to cool slightly, and then remove the flesh from the bone.

8. Heat the tacos for a few seconds on each side, until they become pliable. Divide the tacos between two plates then top with the trout, soured cream, avocado, salted ricotta and pickled onion mixture. Sprinkle each taco with the coriander and then serve with the lime wedges.

GRILLED SALMON OR SEA BASS
WILL ALSO WORK WELL WITH
THIS RECIPE; YOU MAY NEED
TO ADJUST THE COOKING
TIMES SLIGHTLY.

Grilled Lobster
with Nam Jim Sauce

SERVES 2

PREP: 25 MINS + FREEZING

COOK: 20 MINS

INGREDIENTS

2 whole live lobsters, each weighing 675 g/1 lb 8 oz

55 g/2 oz salted butter, melted

1 tsp pepper

NAM JIM SAUCE

small bunch of fresh coriander

10 green bird's eye chillies

½ tsp salt

55 g/2 oz palm sugar

juice of 4 limes

1. Place the lobsters in the freezer for 2 hours before cooking. Bring a large saucepan of salted water to the boil and add the lobsters. Blanch for 5 minutes, then remove and place in iced water for 10 minutes.

2. Cut the lobsters in half lengthways and remove the stomach sack at the head of the lobster. If there is one, remove the black line from the tail of the lobster and any roe in the head area. Crack the claws; this will allow heat in when cooking.

3. Prepare the barbecue for direct cooking and preheat to medium-hot.

4. To make the nam jim sauce, place the coriander, chillies and salt in a food processor. Blend for 30 seconds, then scrape down the sides with a spatula to avoid any lumps. With the motor running, add the palm sugar and lime juice and blend until smooth. Place the sauce in a small bowl.

5. Brush the flesh side of the lobsters with the melted butter and sprinkle with pepper. Place the lobsters, flesh-side down, on the barbecue grill and cook for 5 minutes. Turn over and cook for another 5 minutes, brushing with butter again. When the lobsters are cooked through, serve with the nam jim sauce.

BLANCHING THE LOBSTERS WILL
PREVENT ANY NASTY SURPRISES
OF UNCOOKED CLAW MEAT ONCE YOU
HAVE BARBECUED THEM.

Clams with Smoked Bacon

SERVES 2

PREP: 15 MINS + SOAKING

COOK: 15 MINS

INGREDIENTS

1 kg/2 lb 4 oz fresh clams, scrubbed

SMOKED BACON BUTTER

200 g/7 oz butter

2 shallots, finely diced

2 garlic cloves, finely chopped

100 g/3½ oz smoked bacon lardons

juice of 1 lemon

small bunch of fresh flat-leaf parsley, chopped

1. Soak the clams in fresh water for at least an hour before cooking, then remove from the water and drain well. Discard any clams with broken shells and any that refuse to close when tapped.

2. Prepare the barbecue for direct cooking and preheat to hot.

3. Melt the butter in a large frying pan over a medium heat. Add the shallots, garlic and smoked bacon and cook for 8—10 minutes, or until browned. Remove from the heat and add the lemon and parsley. Set aside in a warm place.

4. Place the clams on the barbecue grill and cook for 4—5 minutes, or until the clams have fully opened. Discard any clams that have not opened at this point.

5. Mix the cooked clams in the bacon butter and serve immediately.

FOR THOSE OF YOU WHO LIKE
THINGS A LITTLE SPICIER, TRY
ADDING A TABLESPOON OF CURRY
POWDER TO THE BACON BUTTER.

Chapter 6
SIDES, DRINKS & DESSERTS

Celeriac, Fennel & Peach Slaw

INGREDIENTS

4 tbsp mayonnaise

1 tsp sriracha chilli sauce

1 tsp horseradish sauce

juice and zest of 1 lemon

½ tsp pepper

2 ripe peaches, stoned and sliced

200 g/7 oz celeriac, cut into matchsticks

1 fennel bulb, sliced

1 small red onion, sliced

1. In a large bowl, whisk together the mayonnaise, chilli sauce, horseradish sauce, lemon zest, lemon juice and pepper.

2. Add the peaches, celeriac, fennel and onion to the bowl.

3. Mix well to combine thoroughly and then serve immediately.

THIS SLAW WILL WORK WELL
WITH ANY STONED FRUIT AND
IS GREAT SERVED WITH PORK,
CHICKEN OR FISH.

Smoky BBQ Beans

SERVES 4

PREP: 10 MINS

COOK: 30 MINS

INGREDIENTS

4 tbsp olive oil

1 large onion, chopped

2 garlic cloves, chopped

2 celery sticks, chopped

1 large carrot, chopped

1 tsp fennel seeds

2 tsp dried oregano

2 tsp smoked paprika

1 tbsp chipotle paste

1 tbsp treacle

450 ml/16 fl oz passata

400 g/14 oz canned cannellini beans, drained and rinsed

salt and pepper

1. Heat the oil in a large saucepan over a medium heat. Add the onion, garlic, celery and carrot and sweat with a lid on for 15 minutes, or until translucent and softened.

2. Add the fennel seeds, oregano, paprika, chipotle and treacle. Cook for 5 minutes to allow the sugars to start to caramelize.

3. Add the passata and beans and cook for a further 10 minutes.

4. Season to taste and serve.

FOR THE MEAT-LOVING
CARNIVORE, TRY ADDING
SMOKED BACON OR CHORIZO.

Home-made Tomato
Ketchup

MAKES 250 ML/9 FL OZ

PREP: 10 MINS

COOK: 15-20 MINS

INGREDIENTS

2 tbsp olive oil

1 red onion, chopped

2 garlic cloves, chopped

250 g/9 oz plum tomatoes, chopped

250 g/9 oz canned chopped tomatoes

½ tsp ground ginger

½ tsp chilli powder

40 g/1½ oz dark brown sugar

100 ml/3½ fl oz red wine vinegar

salt and pepper

1. Heat the olive oil in a large saucepan and add the onion, garlic and all of the tomatoes. Add the ginger and chilli and season with salt and pepper to taste. Cook for 15 minutes, or until soft.

2. Pour the mixture into a food processor or blender and blend well. Sieve thoroughly to remove all the seeds. Return the mixture to the pan and add the sugar and vinegar. Return to the boil and cook until it is the consistency of ketchup.

3. Bottle quickly in sterilized bottles or jars and store in a cool place or refrigerator until required.

THIS HOME-MADE VERSION OF THE TRADITIONAL SAUCE IS MUCH MORE FLAVOURSOME THAN SHOP BOUGHT.

Mayonnaise

☆ MAKES 300 ML/10 FL OZ ☆

PREP: 10 MINS

COOK: NO COOKING

INGREDIENTS

2 large egg yolks

2 tsp Dijon mustard

¾ tsp salt, or to taste

2 tbsp lemon juice or white wine vinegar, plus extra if needed

about 300 ml/10 fl oz sunflower oil

white pepper

1. Whizz the egg yolks with the Dijon mustard, salt and white pepper to taste in a food processor, blender or by hand. Add the lemon juice and whizz again.

2. With the motor still running, add the oil, drop by drop at first. When the sauce begins to thicken, the oil can then be added in a slow, steady stream. Taste and adjust the seasoning with extra salt, pepper and lemon juice if necessary. If the sauce seems too thick, slowly add 1 tablespoon of hot water or lemon juice.

3. Use at once or store in a sterilized and airtight container in the refrigerator for up to 1 week.

THIS RICH AND CREAMY MAYONNAISE IS THE PERFECT ACCOMPANIMENT TO ANY BURGER OR SANDWICH.

Classic BBQ Sauce

☆ MAKES 900 ML/1½ PINTS ☆

PREP: 10 MINS

COOK: 50 MINS

INGREDIENTS

1 small onion

2 garlic cloves

1 tbsp olive oil

225 ml/8 fl oz tomato ketchup

450 ml/16 fl oz passata

100 g/3½ oz brown sugar

4 tbsp cider vinegar

2 tbsp Worcestershire sauce

½–1 tsp cayenne pepper

½–1 tsp smoked paprika or ground chipotle powder

1. Put the onion and garlic into a food processor and purée.

2. Heat the oil in a heavy-based frying pan over a medium-high heat. Add the onion-garlic purée and cook, stirring frequently, until it begins to brown.

3. Add the remaining ingredients and bring to the boil. Reduce the heat to medium and simmer for about 45 minutes, stirring occasionally, until the sauce thickens and begins to darken. Bottle quickly in sterilized bottles or jars and store in a cool place or refrigerator until required.

THIS CLASSIC SAUCE CAN BE USED AS A CONDIMENT WITH ANY MEAT DISH OR YOU CAN ALSO USE IT TO MARINATE BEEF OR PORK BEFORE GRILLING.

Fresh Lemonade

PREP: 15 MINS + STANDING

COOK: NO COOKING

INGREDIENTS

4 large lemons, preferably unwaxed

175 g/6 oz caster sugar

900 ml/1½ pints boiling water

ice cubes

1. Scrub the lemons well, then dry. Using a vegetable peeler, pare three of the lemons very thinly. Place the peel in a large jug or basin, add the sugar and boiling water and stir well until the sugar has dissolved. Cover the jug and leave to stand for at least 3 hours, stirring occasionally. Meanwhile, squeeze the juice from the three lemons and reserve.

2. Remove and discard the lemon peel and stir in the reserved lemon juice. Thinly slice the remaining lemon and cut the slices in half. Add to the lemonade together with the ice cubes. Stir and serve immediately.

YOU CAN TRY USING ORANGES OR LIMES OR ALL THREE FRUITS FOR SOME EQUALLY REFRESHING THIRST QUENCHERS.

Port & Stout Cocktail

SERVES 2

PREP: 5 MINS

COOK: NO COOKING

INGREDIENTS

25 ml/1 fl oz port

150 ml/5 fl oz stout

200 ml/7 fl oz ginger beer

dash of orange Angostura bitters

ice cubes

1. Pour the port, stout, ginger beer and bitters into a cocktail shaker.

2. Top with ice cubes, put the lid on and shake the cocktail vigorously.

3. Pour over ice into two glasses and serve.

THIS RECIPE MAKES A GREAT PUNCH. JUST INCREASE THE QUANTITIES AND ADD A FEW ORANGE SLICES.

Salty Dog

SERVES 1

PREP: 5 MINS

COOK: NO COOKING

INGREDIENTS

1 tbsp granulated sugar

1 tbsp coarse salt

1 lime wedge

cracked ice cubes

50 ml/2 fl oz vodka

grapefruit juice, to taste

1. Mix the sugar and salt in a saucer.

2. Rub the rim of a chilled cocktail glass with the lime wedge.

3. Dip into the sugar and salt mixture, to coat.

4. Fill the glass with cracked ice cubes and pour over the vodka. Top up with the grapefruit juice and stir.

5. Serve immediately.

THE SHARP FLAVOURS OF THE GRAPEFRUIT JUICE AND VODKA COMBINE BEAUTIFULLY WITH THE SUGAR AND SALT.

Grilled Bourbon Peaches

 SERVES 4

 PREP: 15 MINS

 COOK: 20 MINS

INGREDIENTS

6 ripe peaches, stoned and halved

1 tbsp oil

4 tbsp good-quality bourbon

100 g/3½ oz butter

150 g/5½ oz dark brown sugar

1 tsp vanilla extract

150 ml/5 fl oz apple juice

vanilla ice cream, to serve

1. Prepare the barbecue for direct cooking and preheat to hot.

2. Brush the flesh side of the peach halves with the oil.

3. In a saucepan over a high heat, flambé the bourbon then add the butter, sugar, vanilla and apple juice. Bring to a simmer and let everything dissolve and turn slightly syrupy. Remove from the heat and leave to cool.

4. Lay the peaches, skin-side down, on the barbecue grill and cook for 2 minutes, or until the skin starts to char. Carefully turn over with a palette knife and cook for a further 2 minutes.

5. Remove the peaches from the barbecue and serve with ice cream and the bourbon syrup.

TRY THIS RECIPE WITH
A MIXTURE OF STONE FRUIT
AND USE RUM INSTEAD
OF BOURBON.

Fruit Skewers

 SERVES 4

 PREP: 15 MINS

 COOK: 5-10 MINS

INGREDIENTS

a selection of fruit, such as apricots, peaches, strawberries, mangoes, pineapple and bananas, prepared and cut into chunks

2 tbsp maple syrup, plus extra for drizzling

50 g/1¾ oz plain chocolate (optional)

1. Prepare the barbecue for direct cooking and preheat to medium-hot.

2. Thread alternate pieces of fruit onto four pre-soaked wooden skewers or metal skewers. Brush the fruit with the maple syrup.

3. Put the chocolate, if using, in a heatproof bowl. Set the bowl over a saucepan of barely simmering water and stir until the chocolate has completely melted.

4. Place the skewers on the barbecue grill and cook for 3 minutes, or until caramelized. Transfer to serving plates and serve immediately, drizzled with the melted chocolate, if using, and maple syrup.

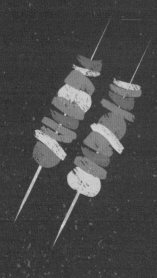

THESE SKEWERS COULD ALSO BE
SERVED WITH LOW-FAT FROMAGE
FRAIS, RATHER THAN THE
MELTED CHOCOLATE.

INDEX

aubergines
  Grilled Cajun Vegetables with
    Parmesan Grits 24
  Mediterranean Grilled
    Aubergines 26
bacon
  Bacon-wrapped Chicken Burger
    with Grilled Pineapple 94
  Clams with Smoked Bacon 108
  Creamed Spinach 36
beans
  Chuck Steak with Black Bean
    Salsa 44
  Smoky BBQ Beans 114
beef
  Beef Brisket with Soy & Ginger
    Rub 40
  Beef Rib Cutlets with Caper &
    Anchovy Butter 42
  Beef Sausages with Scorched
    Tomato Relish 56
  Brined & Smoked Beef Short Ribs
    46
  Brisket Cheesesteak Subs 54
  Cheddar-Jalapeño Beef Burgers
    52
  Chilli Hot Dogs with Texan
    Chilli 68
  Chuck Steak with Black Bean
    Salsa 44
  Porterhouse Steak in Red Wine
    Sauce 50
  Rib-eye Steak with Ranch
    Dressing 48
burgers
  Bacon-wrapped Chicken Burger
    with Grilled Pineapple 94
  Cheddar-Jalapeño Beef Burgers
    52
  Lamb Burgers with Tzatziki &
    Feta 74
  Squash & Polenta Burgers 28
celeriac
  Celeriac, Fennel & Peach Slaw
    112
  Creamed Spinach 36
  Squash & Polenta Burgers 28
cheese
  Baked Sweet Potatoes with Salsa
    34
  Brisket Cheesesteak Subs 54
  Cheddar & Dill Pickle Stuffed
    Jackets 20
  Cheddar-Jalapeño Beef Burgers
    52
  Grilled Cajun Vegetables with
    Parmesan Grits 24
  Grilled Stuffed Peppers 32
  Lamb Burgers with Tzatziki &
    Feta 74
  Pork Meatball Skewers with
    Smoked Cheese Sauce 72
  Portobello Mushrooms 22
  Squash & Polenta Burgers 28
chicken
  Ancho Chilli, Vanilla & Cola
    Chicken 86

Bacon-wrapped Chicken Burger
    with Grilled Pineapple 94
  BBQ Chicken Wings 82
  Chicken Drumsticks with Satay
    Glaze 84
  Sticky Bourbon Chicken Wings 80
  Teriyaki Chicken Skewers 92
chickpeas: Grilled Stuffed
    Peppers 32
Clams with Smoked Bacon 108
courgettes
  Grilled Cajun Vegetables with
    Parmesan Grits 24
  Grilled Stuffed Peppers 32
drinks
  Fresh Lemonade 120
  Port & Stout Cocktail 122
  Salty Dog 123
fennel
  Braised Pork Belly with Apple &
    Mustard Ketchup 64
  Celeriac, Fennel & Peach Slaw
    112
Fruit Skewers 126
lamb
  Lamb Burgers with Tzatziki &
    Feta 74
  Lamb Kebabs 76
Lobster, Grilled, with Nam Jim
    Sauce 106
mayo
  Anchovy Mayo 102
  Mayonnaise 117
Mushrooms, Portobello 22
peaches
  Celeriac, Fennel & Peach Slaw
    112
  Fruit Skewers 126
  Grilled Bourbon Peaches 124
peppers
  Beef Sausages with Scorched
    Tomato Relish 56
  Brisket Cheesesteak Subs 54
  Chuck Steak with Black Bean
    Salsa 44
  Grilled Cajun Vegetables with
    Parmesan Grits 24
  Grilled Stuffed Peppers 32
  Italian Sausage Subs with
    Peppers & Onions 70
pineapple
  Bacon-wrapped Chicken Burger
    with Grilled Pineapple 94
  Fruit Skewers 126
pork
  Braised Pork Belly with Apple &
    Mustard Ketchup 64
  Chilli Hot Dogs with Texan
    Chilli 68
  Italian Sausage Subs with
    Peppers & Onions 70
  Pork Belly Sliders with Kimchi
    Slaw 66
  Pork Meatball Skewers with
    Smoked Cheese Sauce 72
  Pulled Pork with Sweet Potato
    Mash 60

Spicy Baby Back Ribs 62
potatoes: Cheddar & Dill Pickle
    Stuffed Jackets 20
prawns: Whole Grilled Prawns in
    Maple & Sriracha Butter 98
sauces & relishes
  Ancho Chilli Sauce 86
  Apple & Mustard Ketchup 64
  Classic BBQ Sauce 118
  Home-made Tomato Ketchup 116
  Hot Soy Sauce 100
  Nam Jim Sauce 106
  Satay Sauce 30
  Scorched Tomato Relish 56
  Smoked Cheese Sauce 72
  Teriyaki Sauce 92
  see also mayo
sausages
  Beef Sausages with Scorched
    Tomato Relish 56
  Chilli Hot Dogs with Texan
    Chilli 68
  Italian Sausage Subs with
    Peppers & Onions 70
Scallops with Hot Soy Sauce 100
skewers
  Fruit Skewers 126
  Lamb Kebabs 76
  Pork Meatball Skewers with
    Smoked Cheese Sauce 72
  Teriyaki Chicken Skewers 92
slaws
  Celeriac, Fennel & Peach Slaw
    112
  Kimchi Slaw 66
Spinach, Creamed 36
Squash & Polenta Burgers 28
sweet potatoes
  Baked Sweet Potatoes with Salsa
    34
  Pulled Pork with Sweet Potato
    Mash 60
sweetcorn
  Chuck Steak with Black Bean
    Salsa 44
  Grilled Cajun Vegetables with
    Parmesan Grits 24
tofu: Satay Tofu Salad 30
tomatoes
  Ancho Chilli, Vanilla & Cola
    Chicken 86
  Baked Sweet Potatoes with Salsa
    34
  Beef Sausages with Scorched
    Tomato Relish 56
  Chilli Hot Dogs with Texan
    Chilli 68
  Classic BBQ Sauce 118
  Home-made Tomato Ketchup 116
  Smoky BBQ Beans 114
trout: Grilled Trout Tacos 104
tuna: Peppered Tuna Steaks with
    Anchovy Mayo 102
turkey
  Honey & Orange Turkey Breast 88
  Turkey Drumsticks with Mexican
    Spice Rub 90